OTIS TAYLOR

THE NEED TO WIN

BY
OTIS TAYLOR

WITH
MARK STALLARD

www.sportspublishingllc.com

© 2003 Otis Taylor and Mark Stallard
All Rights Reserved.

Director of production: Susan M. Moyer
Developmental editor: Erin Linden-Levy
Book design, senior project manager: Jennifer L. Polson
Dust jacket design: Joseph Brumleve
Copy editors: Cynthia L. McNew and Susan M. Moyer

ISBN: 1-58261-540-3

Printed in the United States.

Dedicated to the loving memory
of my mother and father.

ACKNOWLEDGMENTS

The authors would like to gratefully extend recognition and thanks to everyone who provided help, information, insight and humor in the piecing together of the moments from Otis's life.

Special thanks to Otis's Chiefs teammates: Bobby Bell, Ed Budde, Chris Burford, Len Dawson, Mike Garrett, Dave Hill, Jim Kearney, Mike Livingston, Jim Marsalis, Curtis McClinton, Frank Pitts, Ed Podolak, Gloster Richardson and Fred "The Hammer" Williamson.

Thanks and congratulations to Hank Stram for his insights and on his induction into the Pro Football Hall of Fame. And to Lloyd "The Judge" Wells, who provided priceless information.

Erin Linden-Levy, Cindy McNew, Joseph Brumleve, Jenn Polson, Mike Pearson, Joe Bannon, Jr. and Scott Rauguth of Sports Publishing were terrific. Thanks for believing in the project and helping it become a reality.

Thanks to the Pro Football Hall of Fame Research Library in Canton, specifically Saleem Choudhry, who answered questions and supplied a great deal of material on Otis's professional career and pointed us in the right direction to find other items. The Chiefs' public relations department assisted us a great deal, specifically Morgan Shaw and Pete Moris, supplying needed photos and other information.

Jan Johnson and Alice Ellison at Blue Cross and Blue Shield of Kansas City were helpful and patient.

As with previous projects, Keith Zimmerman and Matt Fulks once again provided major contributions—thanks guys.

And, of course, thanks to our families: Regina Hill Taylor, Florence Odell Taylor, Otis Taylor III, and Merrie Jo Stallard, for your support, help and love.

CONTENTS

Foreword		vi
Introduction		ix
1	From My Own Heart	1
2	The Mama's Boy	11
3	"What's the Matter with You?"	27
4	The Babysitting Caper	41
5	Goin' to Kansas City	52
6	Hammered	73
7	Tumultuous Times	88
8	"That's My Baby!"	106
9	The "Fight"	124
10	All I Want for Christmas . . .	137
11	The Old Pro	151
12	The Talent Scout	180
13	A People Person	195
14	Winning	203
Stats		211

FOREWORD BY LEN DAWSON

When I think about Otis Taylor, the thing that first comes to mind is the term "big-play" performer. He was a clutch player. Otis had so much ability that he was truly a complete football player—not just a guy who could catch the ball.

Otis was one of the first big, sprinter-type receivers. When he came out of college he was about 6'3" and weighed around 220 pounds. He had outstanding speed and athletic ability. Receivers at that time were not that big. A prototypical receiver in those days was Lance Alworth—six feet tall, 185 pounds with good speed. Otis, with his size, was capable of playing tight end, but he had the speed of a receiver.

When I first saw him play, I couldn't get over the wealth of natural ability that he possessed. He had tremendous raw talent. In him I saw a determination to excel. A lot of guys have great abilities, but they don't always make the attempt to excel. Otis did.

Otis was a guy who wanted the ball on every down. I look back at all the big plays that we had in our championship games and Super Bowl games, and Otis was the guy making those plays. He meant a tremendous amount to his teammates, the Chiefs' organization and its early success. In the year of Super Bowl IV, he came up big against the defending champion New York Jets. In the American Football League (AFL) championship game against the Raiders, Otis made the big play. In those days, defenses of the championship teams were so tough and the games were so low-scoring that somebody on offense had to come up with the big play. The most logical guy for us was Otis Taylor.

The big play that most Chiefs fans remember best is the catch Otis made for a touchdown in Super Bowl IV. There are a ton of other catches and big plays that I recall him making, though. He made a remarkable catch against the New England (then Boston) Patriots in old Municipal Stadium. I was intentionally throwing the ball out of the end zone to avoid getting sacked, and Otis reached up with one hand while keeping his feet in bounds and caught that crazy thing. I was just trying to throw the ball away, which is something I didn't admit for a long time; instead, I always said that I was throwing it there because it was the only place where Otis could get the ball without it being intercepted. Otis used to practice catching the ball with one hand, so it shouldn't have been strange that he made that play against the Patriots.

Playing alongside Otis with his wonderful ability gave me a tremendous amount of confidence as a quarterback. I knew that if Otis was in a one-on-one situation and it became a jump ball, I liked his chances of coming up with the catch. He had great leaping ability and could accurately time the ball. I think the fact that he was also an outstanding basketball player helped in that respect. There were times when I took a chance at throwing into a crowd with Otis that I would not have taken with somebody else, because I had faith that if he couldn't catch it, the defense wasn't going to either.

The quarterback-receiver bond that Otis and I shared may never be seen again. Quarterbacks today aren't able to work with receivers the way I was able to work with our receivers, because most of the plays today are called from the sidelines. Every Friday the receivers and I would go over what they thought they could do against that week's opponent. We did a lot of play-action passing, so consequently my back was to the line of scrimmage much of the time. I depended on the receivers to tell me what those defenses were doing once the ball was snapped. It was a different era back then, and the players, in my opinion, were much more involved in the game plan than they are today.

Never afraid to improvise plays, Otis Taylor and Len Dawson frequently discussed strategy during game situations. (Photo provided by the Kansas City Chiefs)

From working closely together, I knew a lot of Otis's moves and he knew mine, as well. Without talking, he knew what I needed on a particular play and I knew where he was going to be. Otis, like our other receivers, was very much a part of molding our offense.

That relationship has carried on since our playing days. Away from the field, Otis has always been a very caring person. He cares about friendships. Once you're a friend of his, you're a friend, period. He does whatever he can to help someone in need. And he does a lot for the community.

When people talk to me about Otis, I'm often asked if he should be in the Pro Football Hall of Fame. Even if Otis and I were not friends, my answer would be the same. Without question, Otis Taylor deserves to be in the Pro Football Hall of Fame. Unfortunately, I think the powers that be are more concerned about a player's numbers than his overall ability. Any receiver can make a lot of catches in his career, but how many of those were significant?

Otis certainly had the numbers, especially based on our offense. We just didn't throw the ball that much—in the neighborhood of 20-25 times a game. Think what he would do in today's offenses, where teams throw the ball 50 times a game! Still, he gained more yards in his career (7,306) than any other receiver in Chiefs history.

Also keep in mind that bump-and-run press coverage was in force when Otis played. In fact, a defender could practically undress the receiver until the ball was in the air, and it was legal. Otis was very good at handling the bump-and-run because of his size compared to the defensive backs. Most of the backs were about six feet tall and weighed less than 190 pounds. The only defensive back who was comparable to Otis in size was Willie Brown. Brown dominated every receiver in the league except Otis. Yes, on his ability and what he contributed to our teams, Otis deserves to be in the Hall of Fame. Looking at the other players of the era, he was as good as any of them—heck, he was better than most of them.

In the pages that follow, you're going to have a chance to learn firsthand about this remarkable athlete, what helped turn Otis Taylor into—arguably—one of the best receivers in the history of football, and why he has *The Need to Win*.

INTRODUCTION

Time does many things. It can enhance good memories, heal bad wounds, exaggerate truths and expand lies. In the world of professional sports, time can over-emphasize an athlete's importance, or sadly, render him lost forever in the dusty archives of forgotten games. Otis Taylor seems to be the paradox; his talent and receiving skills have never been over-exaggerated, and he's certainly not forgotten. But somewhere in between those two very different circumstances, Otis has been placed in a kind of sports purgatory—he was deemed one of the best flankers ever during his playing days, but not in his retirement years.

And it's not fair.

Everyone has seen his spectacular 46-yard catch and run for a touchdown in Super Bowl IV against the Vikings. A great moment, but also symbolic of the plays Otis produced game after game, season after season, for the duration of his career. He could do anything with a football: dance away and around, juke would-be tacklers like a running back, smash into unassuming defensive backs with the bullishness of a fullback, sprint with the speed of a lightning-fast receiver, hammer into linebackers with savage, back-cracking blocks and, of course, catch passes with soft, sticky hands. Otis made impossible catches look easy and turned routine receptions into touchdowns, all the while performing with a powerful style the likes of which pro football had never seen before.

I first met Otis in the fall of 1999, and it was quite a thrill for me because he was one of my favorite sports heroes when I was young. I knew number 89 with the Chiefs was one of the game's special players. One thing I never understood was why the Chiefs didn't throw to him all the time—he appeared to be unstoppable. When we met, I liked him immediately, and he ended up doing the foreword for my *Kansas City Chiefs Encyclopedia*. About a year later, Otis asked me if I would collaborate with him on this book. I quickly accepted.

Otis trusted me from day one as we started the task of compiling his life story. I learned of his wonderful mother, his outstanding high school and college athletic triumphs, and his best and worst moments with the Chiefs. But one sour note kept popping up as we worked. In our research, when we interviewed his friends and former teammates or when he met new people at functions, everyone asked the same question:

"Why isn't Otis Taylor in the Hall of Fame?"

Otis has heard about the Hall of Fame—about not being in the Hall—too much. He hears haunting reminders, almost daily, that he has yet to receive pro football's greatest individual honor. He has no say in the matter, of course, but still he's asked, as if it were up to him whether or not he's ultimately inducted with the other football immortals at Canton.

I've heard all the arguments against Otis being in the Hall of Fame: He didn't play in enough games, didn't catch enough passes, didn't gain enough yards. But if numbers are a major factor for induction, consider this comparison with Lynn Swann, the Steelers' great Hall of Fame receiver: Otis played in more games, caught more passes, scored more touchdowns, gained more yards and averaged more yards per catch than Swann.

Here's another comparison, a simplified look at one of Otis's contemporaries, Hall of Fame running back Gale Sayers. Both men were drafted by the Chiefs in 1965, but Sayers opted for the NFL's Bears, where he played just three complete seasons (68 games total), gained a thousand yards rushing twice, scored 56 touchdowns, and played on only two winning teams. Knee injuries significantly shortened his career, and he played his last game in 1971. Looking at Sayers from this perspective—numbers and longevity—completely distorts what he really was: arguably the greatest running back in the history of the NFL. Watch just 20 seconds of Sayers's film highlights and you *know* he was great.

So was Otis, who made the most of his play opportunities with Kansas City, maximizing his numbers. Within the ball-control offensive philosophy of Chiefs head coach Hank Stram, I feel he actually achieved more in the area of statistics than he should have. Watching film of Otis *or* looking at his statistics conveys the same message: He was a very special football player. A burning desire to win accompanied his tremendous talent and was the staple of his career. Otis took it personally when the

Chiefs lost because his play was about winning, something Kansas City did consistently year after year throughout his career.

With or without the Hall of Fame heading his list of football accomplishments, Otis Taylor is today what he was more than 30 years ago—one of the best receivers of all time. There wasn't anyone in pro football like Otis before he joined the Chiefs, and there hasn't been anyone like him since—a stylish, powerfully flamboyant receiver who wanted the ball and needed to win for himself and his team.

Mark Stallard
May 2003

1

FROM MY OWN HEART

I've had a recurring dream for the past 20 years, and the scenario is always the same: I'm floating—like a plane or giant bird—through the clouds high above a football stadium, yet still making things happen. I'm wearing a football uniform—a Kansas City Chiefs uniform—and below me I hear the large crowd gasp quietly. They point up at me and shake their heads in disbelief. They think I'm showing off, but I'm not. I'm just being myself, using my talents and abilities to be the best I can and helping my team win.

Expressing myself.

The dream is all about me, Otis Taylor, and I'm smooth and fluid—a winner. I always tried to play in high fashion and with a lot of grace, yet I have no idea how I did it, or where my style came from. Some people plan their actions, but I can't do it. When a pass was thrown and I had to get rid of the cover guy, I'd do something, anything, to get open. I'd do it and hope it was the right move, making catches that sometimes surprised even me. But the moves were never planned. I just ran the field and made things happen.

When I awake from this dream, I'm scared as hell. Scared, because I've been dreaming the same dream for so long and it always stops short of a final conclusion, snuffed out before I have a chance to complete my flight. I'm left with an empty feeling of sadness that is the closest thing to death in sports I know.

In the autumn of 1971, I lived this dream.

It was my seventh season of professional football, and while I've always been proud of what I have accomplished throughout my career, I reached what I feel is the closest I've ever been to football perfection game after game for the duration of that campaign. I felt like I could fly in 1971, and like the Jimi Hendrix song, I felt that I could "kiss the sky." The ball always seemed to be within my reach during that dream season, and when it was, I made the catch. That ball was mine.

Very selfish attitude.

Len Dawson, the Chiefs' great Hall of Fame quarterback throughout my career, threw it to me believing I would catch it—no doubts. Of course I did miss some, but I think that every time he cranked up and threw the ball to me, he felt that I would catch it, the entire team felt I would catch it and the fans thought I would catch it. But I *knew* I would.

The Chiefs had a great team in 1971. Coach Hank Stram opened up the offense, and we threw the ball more than we had in previous seasons. Our defense was as good as it had ever been. I think that team, that group of guys—Dawson, Bobby Bell, Ed Podolak, Willie Lanier, Ed Budde, Jack Rudnay, Emmitt Thomas, Jim Kearney, Elmo Wright, and the others—was better than our Super Bowl championship team in 1969, and that was a great, great team. We thought we were the best team in the NFL in 1971—every single man on the team— and there was never a doubt among the group that the Super Bowl was waiting for us at the end of the year. I knew we had to earn it, but confidence in your abilities and your teammates' and coaches' abilities is part of the battle. We had that confidence.

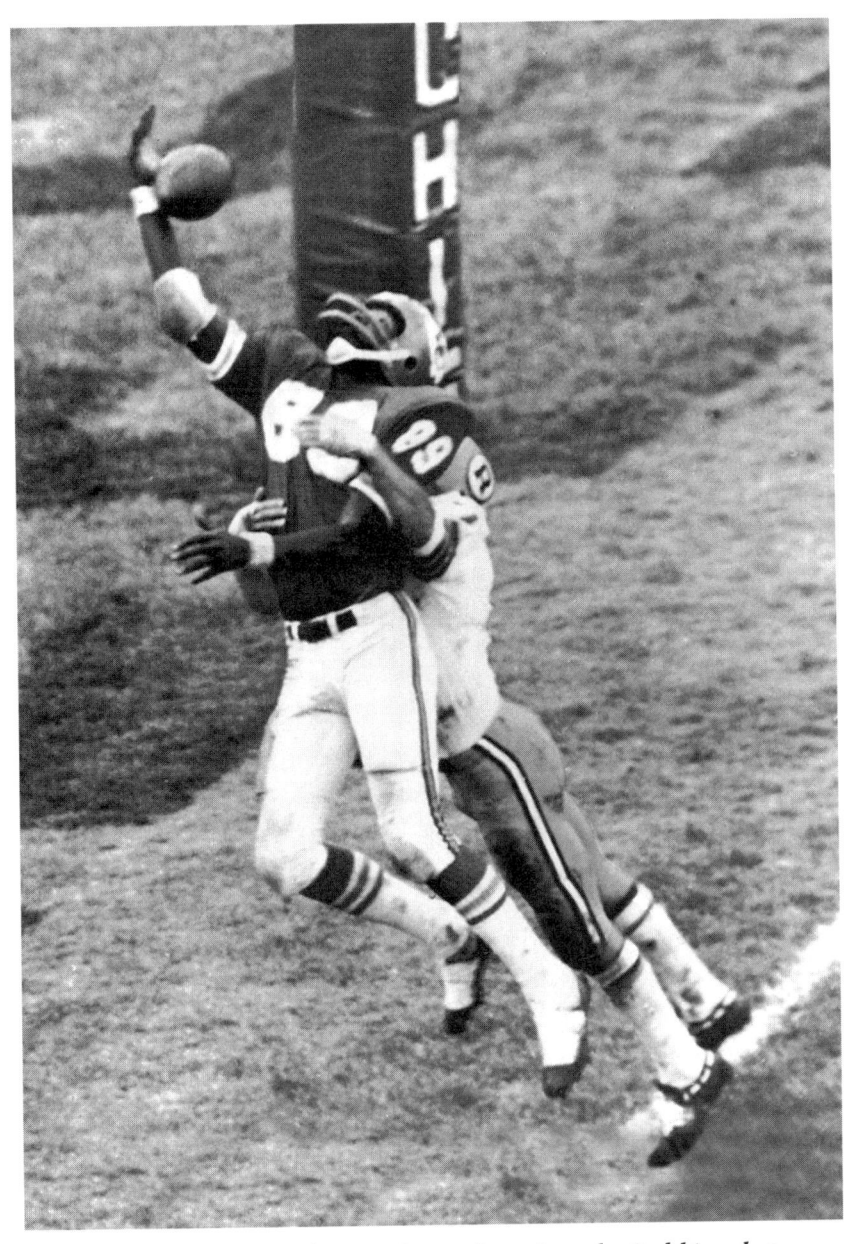

One of my signature photos—the catch against the Redskins that won the game at Municipal Stadium in 1971. That is Washington's tough little defensive back, Pat Fischer, hanging on me. (Photo courtesy of the Taylor Family Collection)

The Chiefs had several big wins that year, defeating Washington, San Francisco, and Pittsburgh. We tied the Raiders in Oakland and defeated them in Kansas City. By season's end we were the Western Division champs of the AFC, finishing with a 10-3-1 record. I compiled some pretty good numbers myself, finishing with 57 receptions for 1,110 yards and seven touchdowns. I even ran one reverse play in for a TD. But the numbers aren't really the story of that season. Whenever the team needed a big play, I made it. When a drive was on the line, Lenny threw to me. If a one-handed catch was the only way I could make the reception, I did it. Dawson threw the ball; I caught it. It was truly a dream season for me personally, and my play was a big reason for the success of the team.

I did experience a mental downside to 1971, however. Whenever I did something during a game that season, like making a diving, one-handed catch, I worried that the fans and media would think I was showing off. It seems ridiculous now, but so many times during the first six years of my career I was wrongly accused of showboating, being lackadaisical, causing team dissension, and generally caring more about myself than the team. So when I made big, spectacular plays in 1971, I worried that the comments would start again.

"Otis had great pride in his talent. And like most great receivers, he liked to catch the ball. We tried to get it to him as much as we possibly could because he was so instrumental in the success of our team. He loved being able to catch the ball and beating the defensive guy one on one—he had speed, grace, style. We also used him as a tight end many times; he was that kind of a player. At that stage of professional football, teams didn't throw the ball like they throw it now. As a result, we didn't get him the ball as much as we would have liked. But we were a great balanced team with a very good running game—Mike Garrett, Eddie Podolak and the other running backs that we had. Our talent was based on the fact that we had to run to win and

we got to throw the ball from play-action passes. We used a lot of play-action passes. And Otis was very instrumental in what we did and how we did it."

—Hank Stram, Kansas City Chiefs Head Coach, 1960-74

My football talent and success came from my own heart. I always played for myself first. I played for the fans, the team, my friends and family, too, but I don't think I would have gotten as much enjoyment out of it if I hadn't played for myself first. Pretty much everything in life—if you want to achieve success—is like that. But before you call me selfish—and I was—consider this: Satchel Paige was selfish. Michael Jordan was selfish. Babe Ruth was selfish. You can't play professional sports and not be selfish, and being selfish doesn't mean that you have to hurt your teammates and the team. I can't play for my teammates, the fans or coaches first, because that kind of thinking would never have allowed me to reach the top of my game and achieve the high standards I set for myself. I was the one catching the ball, running, blocking and scoring the touchdowns. I wanted the cheers of the crowd and the adulation of the fans. That helped me and inspired my play. I always enjoyed the good moments more when they were accompanied by screams of delight and joy for something I did for myself *and* the team. And that always provided me with extra inspiration to catch the next one. But they were still my moments, and I don't think that was hurtful to the team. You have to enjoy it yourself. Do you really think Michael Jordan didn't love to hit those game-winning baskets? Do you think he was making them for somebody else? Or when John Elway was throwing a touchdown pass with three seconds left in a game to win? Was he doing it for somebody else?

It always pissed me off when people—or writers, coaches and teammates—said I was lazy or questioned my desire and work ethic.

I wasn't lazy. I was never lazy. I just did it my way, playing the game the way I played football. I didn't set out to upset the system or go against the coach. I was going to play within the team's system, but I was going to do it my way, whether it was making a block, running a route or catching the football with one hand.

> *"Otis was very serious. Maybe some of the guys had a closer relationship than I had when we were playing, but to me, very candidly, Otis was very intense. He didn't crack those jokes like some of the other guys used to—like Bobby Bell and E. J. Holub. They were kind of like college guys and got the team juiced up, funny and kept everybody loose. But Otis was always a very serious individual."*
>
> —Ed Budde, Chiefs Offensive Guard, 1963-76

The position I played, flanker or wide receiver, is a position that has always been equated with selfishness. I've been called that a million times by coaches, simply because I wanted the ball. That takes a lot of mental toughness and a certain mindset to shake off the criticism, especially when it comes from those closest to you. I knew if the ball was in my hands I could do good things for the team, but you still have to be in tune with yourself, retain confidence in your talent and abilities to let silly and unfair statements like that ride by without hitting back. What a lot of my teammates didn't realize—and some of my coaches, too—was that the "me first" mentality also kept me 100 percent in tune with the team and that I've got to be involved as myself when I'm part of the team to maximize my contributions. Football is a "we" game, but if I do well and make things happen, the coach, system and my teammates will reap the benefits. If I don't do a damn thing, then I can't bring anything to the team. And if you don't do a damn thing, you won't be in the game very long.

"Otis was great on natural ability. This guy was born and tailor-made to be a pass receiver. He had smooth transitional moves from left to right. He could make a cut so quick, you couldn't get there. He had a running style that didn't look like he was running fast, but he would fly past you. I've seen him catch a ball and just run away from guys, and it never seemed liked he was running hard."

—Fred "The Hammer" Williamson,
Chiefs Defensive Back, 1965-67

Like my dream, the 1971 season came to an abrupt, premature end for my teammates and me when we lost to Miami in the infamous double-overtime playoff game on Christmas Day at Kansas City's Municipal Stadium. It was sudden death, and that's exactly how it felt and still feels today. The longest game in the history of the NFL, and what did I contribute to the team? Nothing. I caught three lousy passes for a measly 12 yards. The Dolphins shut me down throughout the game, but our team was so good that we should have won anyway and would have won if Jan Stenerud had hit just one of the three field goals he missed (of the three missed attempts, one was an aborted fake and another was blocked).

The loss to Miami in the 1971 playoff game was especially embarrassing because we had everything. We had the defense and the offense. We had guys who were All-Stars at almost every position, but we didn't lose the thing offensively or defensively. We lost it with special teams. And I say "we" because if we had been in better shape at the end of the game, either by scoring more or giving up less, we wouldn't have had to worry about the overall effect that special teams had on the outcome of the game. I'm not a finger pointer and have never blamed Jan for the loss. I know nobody in the entire Chiefs organization felt worse about the outcome of that game than Jan.

But for that team not to have ended up with a Super Bowl trophy is criminal. That's how good we were.

I did win a few awards following the '71 season, but they were hollow in meaning. The UPI named me the AFC Offensive Player of the Year, *Pro Football Weekly* named me Offensive MVP for the NFL, and I played in my first Pro Bowl (I had played in the AFL All-Star game once before). I'd have traded them all for a shot at the Cowboys in Super Bowl VI.

> *"When you look at a player, you can tell if he's an athlete or not. One look at Otis and you could tell he was an all-around athlete. He probably could have played basketball and probably could have played baseball, too. That's how you tell a good athlete, if a person can do more than one sport. When I met Otis, he was an all-around good sports guy. I knew that he was a player right off the bat, and most people want to be around players. If you walked on the field and he was hurt a little bit, you knew he was still going to give you everything he had. He never had anything left in his tank at the end of the game."*
>
> —Bobby Bell, Chiefs Linebacker, 1963-74

My passion for sports as a whole has always been complete. Football, basketball, baseball, hockey—it's all art to me. You know when someone paints a picture and everything fits perfectly? That's the way sports, and football in particular, are for me. The whistle blows and everything starts—players running, pushing, blocking. It's a moving collage of human art. You have to have a special appreciation for football, and when you've played it before and have been a part of that human collage, you can sit back, look at it and see so much—so many things that are right about a particular play, and also what's wrong. I just care about the game. The only negative thing about football, at least from my playing days, is that I had several knee injuries—the first when I was in high school—as well as a lot of other little things that went wrong or were injured.

I played on a bum knee for four years. I'm living on a bum knee right now. Although I've had my left knee replaced, it's still not close to being 100 percent, but it's better than it was. When I played, I played in pain if I had to, because I didn't want to get off the field. I live in pain today, because I want to keep living and watch other people live.

Throughout my career and afterward, I visited the Children's Mercy Hospital in Kansas City with several different teammates many times, and saw children without hands or arms—kids born without arms. Every time I saw them it hurt. But always, without exception, the faces of those kids would reflect a happiness and joy. Some were on their deathbeds; others knew they would never have arms or hands or other physical attributes in their lives. It made me feel very insignificant because they could smile despite their overwhelming adversities. It also helped me instill a will within myself to look at things in much the same light that those brave children did: not to take anything for granted in my life and look for a happiness that can always be found. I used their brave examples to make my life better and also to excel in football, taking full advantage of my physical gifts. If you really want to get in touch with life, go to a children's hospital and see how brave those kids are. They don't know when their last moments are going to happen, but they're still smiling.

If you haven't already figured it out, I'm an extremely emotional man. Tell me a sad story and I'll get choked up. Talk to me about some of the injustices that plague American life today and I'll get angry. Share a warm moment from your past, or ask me about one of mine—especially if it deals with my mother—and I'll probably cry. That's me. I never held back these emotions on the football field, and I've never held them back in life.

> *"Otis had a great ability to put people at ease and make fun of himself and people around him in a way that made everybody feel comfortable. A lot of times he used the coaching staff as the butt of his jokes. It ended up being funny for everybody and kept the team together."*
>
> —Ed Podolak, Chiefs Running Back, 1969-77

Was I a good receiver? Yes, and I don't just think it; I know it. But I also know I could have been better. If I missed the ball, a crucial reception, I beat myself up long after the game. I always felt as if I had let the team down and let *myself* down. But no matter how many problems I had or appeared to cause to those around me, I never copped out on my teammates. I never abandoned the ship. I was at every practice, and if I could walk, I played. I had a couple of bad injuries, but I always wanted to play. I knew more people were riding on my back than I was riding on theirs, and that was okay with me. That's the way I wanted it. I was happy being one of the main weapons for the Chiefs for so many years. Yes, it was selfish, but my success meant success for the Chiefs. That's why my dream scares me so much today, almost haunts me.

I know I did extraordinary things for myself and the team, but I've always felt like I could have done more.

2

THE MAMA'S BOY

I was born on August 8, 1942, in the third ward of the Cuney projects in Houston, Texas. My family lived a three-bedroom apartment, and it was nice. The project itself was fine. I didn't grow up in the depths of poverty; we weren't crammed into dirty, unlivable spaces, and our neighbors were highly respectable people. We were poor, I guess, but I never knew it. I always had clean clothes, good food to eat and security. And what I might have lacked financially was more than made up for with love. If someone has a mother like mine, they have great wealth their entire life and are richer than words can convey.

Lillian Lee Taylor, my mother, possessed an inner strength that amazes me still. Lord, was she strong, and her strength was given to me freely as I grew up. A woman without much education—she didn't finish high school—my mother's knowledge and wisdom came from the simple aspects of everyday life. She was everything to me as I grew up, and her guiding hand and love were the most important things in my life, not only in my childhood, but long after I had become a man.

I was, in short, an out-and-out mama's boy.

Mom and her two babies—Odell, center, is three years old and I'm one. (Photo courtesy of the Taylor Family Collection)

Mother was from Louisiana, and she was everything anyone could want or even imagine having as a mother, rich, poor, black, white—whatever the social or ethnic background. Her family was always first. I know there were many, many times when my mother went without to make things better for me and my sister Odell—way too many times—and I'll never forget her sacrifices. There was never a day in my youth when I came home to a dirty house, and that's saying a lot, considering how many hours she usually worked.

Mother ran the neighborhood. Everybody would say, "There's Mrs. Taylor, we'd better get going." As strong as she was for my sister and me, she still had strength left to give to the neighborhood. Nobody ever went hungry around her. If you came to our house hungry, you wouldn't leave that way. Mother was the best cook, period, and her gumbo was fantastic. Pork chops, steak, gravy, desserts—it was all good, and she loved preparing food and loved feeding her family, friends and neighbors. All of my friends who met and knew mother appreciated her.

Regardless of how much work Mother was doing (and she did something all the time, every day, every hour) I was still a very much attended-to child—a spoiled child. When she went to work, many times Odell and I went with her. She was a domestic worker for a pretty well-off family—the Zubers—and we would sleep in their hallway if we got tired and were waiting to go home. The Zubers adored her, too, and kept paying her long after she retired. They also bought me and Odell clothes and other items. They were like her second family, and she was family to them.

My sister, Florence Odell Taylor, has always been very special to me. Odell—we always called her Odell instead of Florence—watched out for me when I was little, fought a few of my fights for me, and made sure I walked the straight and narrow when Mother wasn't around. A lot of folks thought we were twins—Otis and Odell—but she's 18 months older than me.

Odell and me, ages seven and five. (Photo courtesy of the Taylor Family Collection)

After she graduated from high school, she started working at a hospital in Houston. She became a nurse's aide, moved up the ladder, and stayed 35 years at the same hospital. Sometimes I think that everyone was so worried about giving me what I wanted and needed that we forgot about her. She'll tell you in a minute that's not true, but those are still my feelings. If I could do one thing in my life during my remaining years, it would be to stand up, look at her and tell her how much I love her. She's been so important to me. She does so much for the people around her, and she gets very little in return. But she's one of those types of people—caring for others is her main goal in life.

When Mother was bedridden in her final months before she died about five years ago, Odell was there, taking care of her and making sure she was comfortable. I'll always be grateful to her for that—for making Mother's final days as good as they could be.

"We were poor people, came up the hard way, and lived in a project when we were little. From there Mother bought our first home because Otis wanted to play ball at E. E. Worthing High School. She managed to buy the house paying two notes—a down payment and a note—just to get him in that area so he'd be eligible to play at Worthing. It was hard, but we worked, and Otis worked, too. He sold popcorn and peanuts when he was small and we saved. He's never really been in any trouble; he was a very good boy. I've always been proud of him because he's been such a good person. He played ball, came home, did what he was told to. If he was disciplined or punished, it was something he accepted. I'm just proud that he's my brother."

—Florence Odell Taylor, Otis's Sister

I did the traffic patrol at my grade school. We had an old fishing pole with a red stop signal on it, and we'd let it down so the kids could cross over at intersections around the school. After a couple of years I became the chief of patrol. My mother worked and struggled to buy me the uniform I needed, and I loved it. I loved putting it on and wearing that uniform. That was one of the best gifts I ever got from her because it was so important to me.

The school traffic guard—I always loved uniforms, even at this early age. (Photo courtesy of the Taylor Family Collection)

That's probably when I became a freak about uniforms. As far back I can remember, I've loved uniforms. They've always fascinated me, and I'm drawn to them in general. I think that if I hadn't gone to college or become a professional football player, I would have gone into some branch of the service or been a police officer—someone in a uniform. Even at my age now, whenever I'm at the airport, I enjoy seeing an airline captain in his pressed uniform, looking sharp, with his tie on and his shoes shined. I also like marines in their full dress uniform. Seeing them always makes me feel like sticking out my chest and becoming a part of their organization.

"Otis was small [in size] when he was young, and for a long time he stayed short. He wasn't a big guy. When we went to school together, I would always have to take him to his class because he was a scaredy cat. He was athletic, though, and the men in the neighborhood would come and get him to play football and other sports. The guys would

also razz and tease him, but he wasn't the kind that would talk back for himself. I would always have to do it, even when it came down to fist fights. It's funny, he just never did fight back. He's not a violent person. He's always been like that—real meek—and I was always the one who took care of him."

—Florence Odell Taylor

Every summer Odell and I would take the train to De Quincy, Louisiana, where Mother's sister and daddy lived. My grandpa, John Lee, lived in Abbeville, and we'd go stay there for two or three weeks. The train ride was always a joy and an adventure. Mother would fry a couple of chickens, put them in a bag and we'd eat chicken and drink soda on the train. Riding the train back then—a slow train that stopped at every little town—was exciting. We'd look out the windows at the sights and enjoy the ride. My sister was such a leader; I didn't have to worry about doing anything wrong because she wasn't going to let it happen. The ride to De Quincy and Abbeville was almost as good as the time we spent there.

Every morning at five o'clock during our summers with Grandpa, all the kids in town and the surrounding area—both black and white—would load onto some trucks and head out to pick cotton. But my grandpa would not let me and Odell go. And if you didn't pick cotton, there would be very little to do the rest of the day because everyone was gone. I tried to slip out and go once, and Grandpa told me if I ever did that again I'd be punished. He did not want me picking cotton, so I never did.

"Every summer for about 10 years we went to Louisiana to stay with our aunt. Mother would put us on the train in Houston, and they would get us off the train around 12 o'clock in De Quincy. We would stay there all the summer. Everybody in that town—the working

The gunslinger, age three. (Photo courtesy of the Taylor Family Collection)

men—was a railroad man. It was a good time, because it was usually just Otis and myself. At home we didn't run around the neighborhood very much and usually stayed in the house most of the time. We just didn't get a chance to just run loose in our neighborhood. So we looked forward to going there because my aunt had seven children, and we really enjoyed it."

—Florence Odell Taylor

The first organized team sport I played was baseball, Little League in the summer. And I was a pretty good baseball player, at least that's what a lot of people used to tell me. Besides baseball, I went to the YMCA—it was very close to our home—and I played a lot of baseball and basketball there, too. I used to spend the whole day at the Y in the summer. Mom and Dad would go to work before I'd get up. I'd leave the house at 8:30 or 9:00, and I wouldn't come home again until six or seven o'clock in the evening. That was my routine almost every day in the summer.

When I was old enough, I worked every weekend sacking groceries or at the ballpark selling peanuts and popcorn. I also did little odd jobs to help my mother around the house. When I was a little older I did a lot of caddying and lawn work—anything to make money. When I was in college Mother sent me $5 or $10 periodically, telling me it was for the things I did around the house for her as a boy.

My dad, Otis Taylor Sr., was from Baytown, Texas, a little town outside of Houston. He was a common laborer—custodial work—and he also worked at a steel factory for quite some time. He loved baseball, and he loved talking to people about baseball. I've always considered baseball to be the sport of sports. We liked football, basketball and the others back then, but baseball was really the sport. You might see three or four guys sitting in the neighborhood with a

A happy mama's boy. (Photo courtesy of the Taylor Family Collection)

little drink and listening to the baseball game on the radio, listening intently to the play-by-play. Baseball can bring people together in social settings that otherwise wouldn't exist. So dad was a baseball nut, and he and the guy across the street would sit on the porch and listen to baseball games every night.

One of my favorite memories of Dad is sitting on his lap in his old green Chevy truck, steering. I could hardly see over the steering wheel, but he let me steer and taught me how to shift. He'd say, "Put it up, put it into first." We'd start moving away from the stop sign—I couldn't see what was in front of us—and he'd say, "put it in second" then "put it in third." That's one of the most touching moments I had with him.

Unfortunately, I didn't become real good friends with my dad until late in his life. He had a drinking problem most of his life, but we worked as a family to help Dad because my mom loved him. We cared about each other, and we stayed together. The last few years of his life, I'd slip him $50 whenever I visited him and mom. I told him not to tell Mother or Odell that I gave him money; that it was between the two of us. The money was in case he wanted to buy a little beer. What surprised me the first time I did that was when I returned about six weeks later and he looked around and whispered, "Come here, come here." He reached his hand in his pocket and there was $42 or $47. He said, "I didn't need it all." And I said, "Well, here's $50 more. I won't tell now, but you've got to keep acting right. I don't want Mother calling me and telling me that you're causing problems." It was almost like we were playing a game. I found something that I could do for him that he was probably waiting on for years and years. All I had to do was take my time and think of something for him. I think that before he passed away, he was a changed man.

"Otis had a strong family. His mother was behind him 100 percent. My family was behind me. I guarantee you one thing, I bet that 75 to 80 percent of everybody who is in professional sports has a strong family, whether it's a single-parent home or a more conventional family—family ties are behind them 100 percent. That's because you're looking for your mother and father sitting in the stands."

—Jim Kearney, Chiefs Safety, 1967-75

•••

"When he was about six years old, the guys in the neighborhood would come and get him because he would play—it was mostly football then. Back then they didn't have any organized Little League clubs, just some guys who would get the little guys together and show them how to play football. No helmets, just the football. Mother was always afraid to let him go, thinking he was going to get hurt because he wasn't big, and then all of a sudden, he just grew up. In high school, Otis did it all—track, basketball, football. He was hardly ever at home because a sport was always in season. But he always played football; he really liked football."

—Florence Odell Taylor

I played four sports in high school: football, basketball, baseball and track and field. I enjoyed the notoriety and how sports, if you were good, would make you popular. All through high school I wouldn't get home until six or seven o'clock because of sports, but that never really hampered my studying. I was making Bs and Cs, but

The 1960-61 E. E. Worthing High School basketball team. I'm in the back row, third from the left (No. 52). (Photo courtesy of the Taylor Family Collection)

I never fully applied myself to the class work, which was a mistake. I played football in front of thousands of people weeknights when I was in junior high and high school. It filled me up. I enjoyed playing it because I enjoyed the roar of the crowd and the chants of "Let's go, baby!" and "Let's go, Big O!" I was always very likeable in all the situations that I've ever been in. God's really blessed me with that personality. Teachers used to pick me up and give me a ride to school in bad weather.

By my senior year at E. E. Worthing High, I was being tabbed as one of the greatest, if not the greatest, high school athlete ever in the area. But I was also branded a "bad actor" during high school, and some news items even said I was uncoachable. That was bull. Consider this little tidbit written during my senior year at Worthing High by Bud Johnson, a sportswriter for the *Forward Times* in Houston:

> "For three years, the exploits of Taylor have become almost legendary, but so have stories of his bad temper and surly attitude.
>
> "This writer, however, despite the bad temper, so-called thugish attitude and poor sportsmanship, would like to pay homage to Taylor as the greatest high school athlete of the decade and not Taylor, the bad-tempered boy."

I don't know where this stuff came from. I always got along with my coaches—always followed directions. Did I have a bad temper at times? Maybe, but I certainly never deserved that kind of treatment from the local press. Bud Johnson, who has had a reputation for writing negative articles for more than four decades in Houston, even went so far as to say my "bad attitude" was keeping college recruiters away.

My football coach, John Tankersly, never thought I was much of a problem.

"He's great, all right," Coach Tankersly said my senior year. "The best all-around quarterback in the city. With Otis calling the plays, we should go all the way to the state championship." And my high school principal said, "I believe he is the best in the state. He is also a good student and a four-letter man."

"In high school, Otis did it all. He was hardly ever at home because it was one season to the next. If the sportswriters said he was temperamental and moody, or a problem, it was probably because he wasn't a talker. He was really like my dad. He would answer a question if you

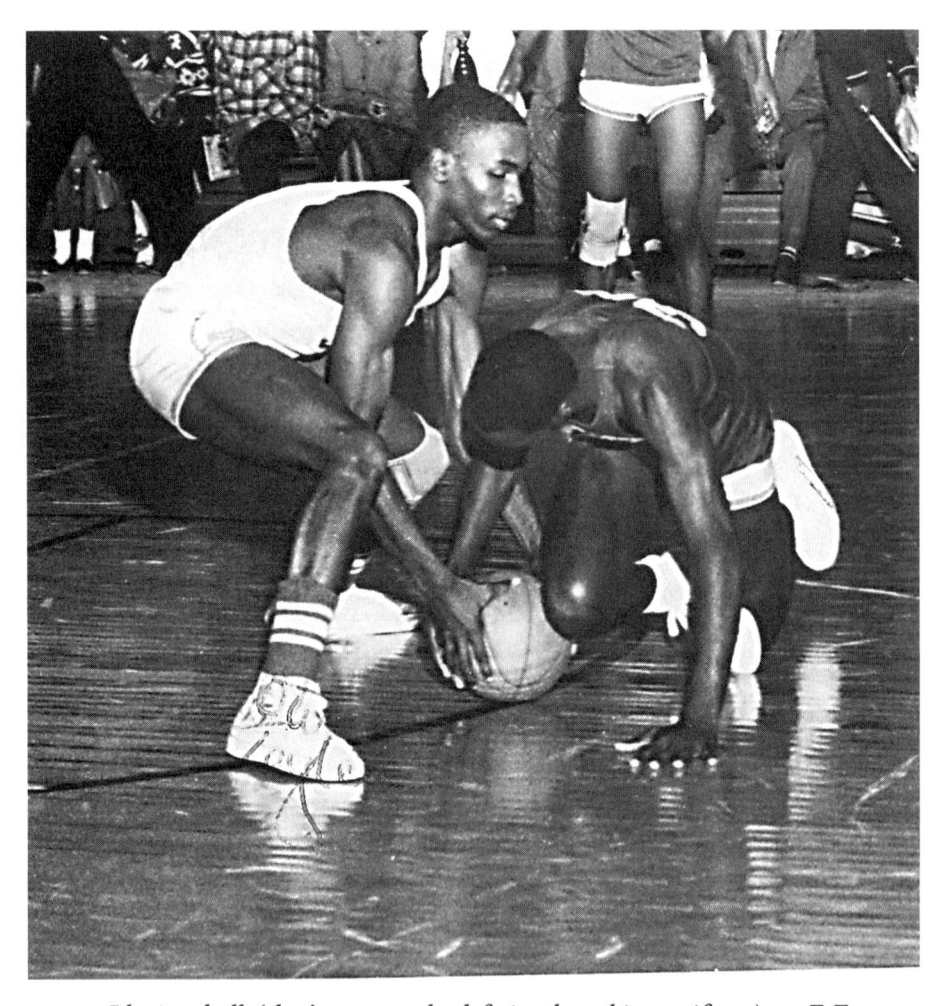

Playing ball (that's me on the left in the white uniform) at E.E. Worthing High during my senior year. (Photo courtesy of the Taylor Family Collection)

would ask him one. If you didn't ask him anything, he didn't say anything. That's how my dad was. Otis was such a quiet person, we sometimes forgot he was in the house."

—Florence Odell Taylor

We went to the winged-T offense my senior year at Worthing and I piled up some pretty impressive numbers at quarterback. The offense was designed to take advantage of my running ability, and it did. In our 58-0 blowout win over Palestine, I scored 28 points (I kicked the extra points) and threw for another six. I returned a punt 35 yards for a score, ran 25 for another, and finished by returning an interception for yet another score. The rest of the season, when I was able to play, went pretty much the same. We didn't win the championship, but we did have a pretty good team.

I was All-City three straight years in all four sports. My basketball coach, Benny Roy, was a good guy. I averaged about 20 points a game my final season, but our team was only average. I was good enough to turn the heads of recruiters.

> *"Otis Taylor is endowed with all the physical attributes an athlete needs in addition to being an excellent shot from anywhere on the court. He is a terrific driver and has a soft touch on his jump shot that has made him as accurate as anyone else, if not more so."*
>
> —Lloyd Wells, *Houston Informer*, February 23, 1960

I was a pretty good pitcher on the ball diamond at Worthing, and I also played a little first base. But I had all kinds of trouble trying to hit curve balls. I could hit it, just not the way I wanted to hit it. I've always thought that because of all the other sports I played, I was never able to practice baseball the way it needs to be done. The sport is too demanding.

I guess I was pretty good in track & field, too. By my senior year, I could long jump 21 feet, toss the shot put close to 50 feet, and high jump six feet, and if that wasn't enough, I also ran the anchor in the 440 relay. My track coach was Clint Williams.

I damaged the ligaments in my left knee my senior year in high school and had an operation that cut into my overall playing time. Throughout my athletic career I was kind of snakebitten, because 90 percent of my injuries were on the left side of my body. Knee, elbow, ankle—every major injury I had was on my left side. Even though I ran the ball and would grip it with my left hand and use my right to ward off defenders with the short-arm upper cut, I hardly ever injured my right hand. Even today, my left side is completely out of sync and my right side feels fine. Believe it or not, I was criticized for not going out of bounds more to avoid hits. I didn't go out of bounds because that wasn't my nature.

There was no way in the world I could go to college without sports. The knee injury not withstanding—and it slowed me considerably—I started to get regular visits from college recruiters midway through the football season. Even though I was "the boy with too much talent and a chip on his shoulder," I would get the opportunity to attend college on an athletic scholarship.

3

"WHAT'S THE MATTER WITH YOU?"

When I was recruited to play college football, I knew I would choose a school from the Southwestern Athletic Conference (SWAC), which was made up of the following schools in the early 1960s: Grambling State, Prairie View A&M, Texas Southern University, Arkansas-Pine Bluff, Alcorn State, Wiley, Southern and Jackson State. I was actually pursued by just a few of the conference's schools, one of which was Texas Southern, and I already knew that I didn't want to go there. Lloyd "The Judge" Wells, a Houston sportswriter and family friend, had followed my career since junior high (he would also play a big part later when I chose the Chiefs) and he knew Prairie View's head coach, Billy Nicks. His little push, and the fact that the school was only 50 miles from home, helped to make the selection easier for me, especially since the number of schools I could attend was limited.

The University of Houston was very close to my house, and I could have virtually walked two blocks to the left and been on their campus. I could have walked two blocks in the opposite direction and been on the Texas Southern campus. But the University of Houston was still segregated in those days—no blacks—and I didn't particularly care for TSU. I wasn't contacted by any schools outside of the SWAC. The large schools in the north, east and west—the USCs, Michigan States, Syracuses and others—never gave me a look. It's just as well; I know I would never have gone that far from home.

As great a reputation as Grambling had—not just in the SWAC, but in the country—I never gave them serious consideration. It was just too far from home. At the time, Grambling had a guy named Tom Williams who brought recruits to their campus. Grambling is in a somewhat isolated place, east of Shreveport, and in those days when you made the final turn off the highway that led to the school, you would see nothing. I mean nothing—no houses, no trees, no barns or livestock. It was just so isolated. It reminds me of when I went to Kansas State University the first time. You take that right turn off I-70 after driving west through Kansas from Kansas City, and then you go about seven or eight miles to get to the K-State campus and there's nothing but wheat. That's the way Grambling was.

When Tom Williams took the recruits home from Grambling, he'd go through New Orleans, telling them how close the school is to the city—it was really about five hours away. Many recruits wouldn't know the difference and sign. I'm sure they never saw New Orleans the entire four years they were there, but it was an effective recruiting mechanism that he used to get them to play for Grambling's great coach, Eddie Robinson. And boy did they have some great players—Buck Buchanan, Willie Brown, Ernie Ladd, Jim Harris (the first black quarterback in the NFL) and Doug Williams, to name a few.

> *"Grambling really wanted Otis, but for some reason he didn't want to go there or to Texas Southern—I don't know why. When the recruiters came by to talk to my mother after school, I would just move on out of the way. It was their business, and she did the talking. They really wanted him at Prairie View and Grambling. I don't think*

Otis wanted to go that far from home, to Grambling, so he decided on Prairie View."

—Florence Odell Taylor

It may sound a little simple, but I ended up right where I wanted to be at Prairie View because I could almost walk home. I felt like if I got into trouble I would be able to get to my mother quickly. I also saw some pretty girls on campus, and that made all of the difference in the world. So I became a Prairie View A&M Panther, wearing their royal purple and gold uniforms for the next four years.

The second oldest public institution in Texas, Prairie View A&M opened in 1876 with a pledge by the state that "separate schools shall be provided for the white and colored children." Prairie View was the solution to the "separate" part. Times have changed, and mostly for the better. The student population in 1961 was almost entirely African American. Today Prairie View is equally split, with as many white kids as black.

Something else is different, too.

When I enrolled there, the school had a tremendous athletic tradition. For the past 20 years or so, the school has had one of the worst football programs in the country. But in 1961, Prairie View was on par with Grambling and every other top power in the small college football world.

My head coach at Prairie View, Billy Nicks, is the winningest coach in the school's history. A College Football Hall of Fame inductee, Coach Nicks's teams won five national championships and eight Southwestern Athletic Conference titles and finished undefeated five times. In 1963 and 1964, my junior and senior seasons, we won the Black College National Championship. I think Coach Nicks ranks up there with some of the great coaches of college football, even though his name isn't widely recognized. Personally, I would rate him about

Seth Cartwright, left, Coach Billy Nicks, center, and me at Prairie View. (Photo courtesy of the Taylor Family Collection)

the same as Hank Stram; their styles and personalities were similar. His coaching staff was small by today's standards—a staff of three with maybe two grad assistants. And we had a trainer. Coach Nicks was also the athletic director, head basketball and baseball coach as well.

A lot of great athletes played for Coach Nicks at Prairie View. Pro Football Hall of Famer Kenny Houston, AFL All-Pro running back Clem Daniels, defensive back Jim Kearney (and my Prairie View teammate) of the Kansas City Chiefs and tight end Alvin Reed of the Houston Oilers.

"Everybody in the SWAC was after him, Southern, Grambling, TSU. But Prairie View's coach, Billy Nicks, was a friend of mine who helped me with my high school All-Star games that I started for black people, and we never had that before. So I pointed Otis to Prairie View."

—Lloyd Wells

One of my neighborhood friends drove me to school the first time because my family didn't have a car then. That was in mid-semester, January 1961, and my first few weeks at Prairie View were tough. I was away from home for the first time and I felt like an outsider on the campus-actually I wasn't letting myself feel a part of it. I was very, very lonesome.

So I quit and went home.

When I got to the house, Mother was waiting for me.

"What's the matter with you?" She always started off by asking that when questioning me about anything. I couldn't give her a legitimate answer because I was scared to death. Scared I was in trouble, scared I had screwed up, and scared because I had let her down. But she knew what was wrong—I was just lonesome for her and my family.

I was still a mama's boy—the baby of the family. A funny thing about that little trip back to Houston and the Sunnyside neighborhood: Everything I had was in a brown paper bag-some khakis and blue jeans, a few nice shirts, penny loafers and tennis shoes. That was my entire wardrobe. I didn't need a lot of clothes because we were in the ROTC at Prairie View, a two-year deal that all students had to participate in. That military uniform was good for making a smaller wardrobe look a lot bigger.

I don't know exactly what I was expecting when I got home. That I would be babied a little? Told not to worry about going to school? I don't remember. Whatever it is I wanted, I didn't get it, because Mother straightened me out—fast. She was not happy and told me it was time for me to become a man—that this was my big chance for success in life. She immediately made me go back to Prairie View. I took my brown bag of clothes and returned to school. I never had another problem about wanting to leave Prairie View again.

"I can remember him coming home a few weeks after he first went to Prairie View. And I can remember him and Mother really getting into it. I don't know if Otis came home because he didn't like being away or if there was something he didn't like at school. But I do remember Mother saying, 'Oh, no, you aren't coming home, not with a scholarship,' and she took him back to Prairie View."

—Florence Odell Taylor

I was never the smartest guy in my classes at Prairie View, but I did okay. And it seemed like all my instructors-and maybe I'm wrong saying this—liked me. I respected them and I think that they respected me as a young man coming from the situation I came from. I seemed to always make a good impression with my instructors, and I always showed them respect and courtesy. I know that helped me a few times get a better grade; a C might become a B if they liked you or a D if you were a jerk to them.

I always let the instructors know when we were playing a game—football or basketball—because many of the teachers thought very little of football. Some of them would ask me how I did in the games, some of them never went to a game, and some of them hated football.

It's hard to please everyone.

A major problem at Prairie View was that I lived in the worst place in the world: the dormitory that housed the football players. We had a rat that lived in the dorm—a huge, monstrous rat the size of a large cat. We named him Big Ben and if you went into the hallway after 9:00 at night, look out. Big Ben patrolled it as if it were his own and scared the hell out of a lot of guys. Sometimes you'd hear loud, startled screams at night.

"Oh, Lord, I saw him!" someone would yell and that big rat would stand up on his hind legs—he had to be more than three feet high—and just dare anyone in the place to cross his path.

Aside from Big Ben, the dormitory was just not a comfortable place to live. It was too hot in the summer-and it could be scorching in the building-and of course too cold in the winter. Not exactly the ideal atmosphere for a championship football team, but we didn't care. In the middle of my junior year, the dorm "mysteriously" burned down. We lost all of our clothes, but were given little provisional checks to buy some new things.

After that they put us in another small, uncomfortable building and we slept two, maybe three guys to a room. The seniors had the option of the third floor, where the best rooms were. My mother used to send me little bags of goodies every other week; cans of Vienna sausages, potted meat, crackers and other stuff. Snack things that I could eat in the room. I'd barely have the bag in my hands before some of the guys, besides my roommates, would show up.

"What'd you get, Otis?" I had to leave the stuff out because I couldn't lock it up—the doors didn't have locks. Share and share alike. In addition to Mom's goody bags, sometimes a group of us would get three fried chickens to split between us, and that's what we'd eat on the weekends.

When we were really hungry and didn't have much to eat, we'd steal watermelons. There was a great watermelon patch in Hempstead, Texas, which was about five miles from the campus-the best watermelons in the world. We'd drive over there, grab a couple of melons apiece, and hope we didn't get caught. The proprietor had a BB gun, and he never hesitated to use it. Scared the hell out of us a few times, shooting that gun at us while ran out of the field with melons under each arm. The stealing wasn't right, but it seemed like we were always hungry, and the dining hall was closed on the weekends.

I had a job because I had to have some supplemental money to live. I worked in the cleaners on a steam presser with steam coming up on me. I did that two days a week. Everything else I needed, books and stuff, was taken care of by my scholarship, which was officially for basketball, not football.

I'd like to say that I was just as good on the basketball court at Prairie View as I was on the football field, but I wasn't. I think I was still pretty good, but inevitably I would be the guy on the team who guarded the opponent's center or big man. The SWAC had good basketball players, too, and I usually ended up playing against guys like Grambling's Willis Reed, the great center who played for the New York Knicks in the 1960s and '70s. The two of us banged heads a few times, and even though I gave away about six inches to Reed, I played him pretty even.

I really enjoyed basketball, though, and if not for football, I think I might have been able to excel more than I did. As it was, I still averaged 17 point a game for my career, which isn't bad. And I'm glad

I had the opportunity to play both sports at Prairie View, which is something very few of today's athletes can or want to do.

> *"Otis was a quarterback when he came to Prairie View, and I was also a quarterback. So at the first practice, Otis is helping me throw the ball, and he's standing there throwing the ball 70 yards. But he no longer wanted to be a quarterback. He wanted to be switched to a wide receiver, and sometimes I wish I had done that move instead of Otis. Still, it was a good move for him."*
>
> —Jim Kearney

We took a bus to all of the away football games and had a great time. Since we usually left at midnight, everybody would sleep most of the trip. Before leaving, we'd circle the campus once and blow the air horn. The bus driver would get settled and we would say, "Bus, give us a run!" The driver would circle the campus and blow it out. He had to do it, or we wouldn't let him leave. The girls would turn on the lights in their dorm, holler and wave at us. It was a major tradition. And since I was one of the hot shots on the team, I rode up where the luggage was with a pillow and a blanket and slept comfortably the whole trip. We'd get to the school we were playing, whichever one it was, at around 6 or 7 o'clock in the morning, go to the gym with our pillows and sleep for a couple of hours before getting something to eat. Most of the games were played in the afternoon and afterwards we'd dress, shower, and come back home. If we won, and we almost always did, the driver would circle the campus when we got back, blowing the horn several times and waking everyone up at two or three in the morning.

> *"Otis was our captain at Prairie View, kind of like our coach on the field. He'd come back to the huddle and say 'Jim, their defensive back*

is doing this, or their defensive back is doing that, and I can beat him on a post pattern, a flag, or a comeback.' Of course we didn't have the computers and charts that all teams use today, and we literally played in a cow field at Prairie View. If I asked Otis to explain the patterns in more detail, he would get down and draw the pattern right in the dirt. We'd been together for so long that I knew the combination was right. That's one of the reasons why Otis made All-American three years in a row. I was All-American three years in a row, too, and Otis was the main reason."

—Jim Kearney

One of my best buddies at Prairie View was Seth Cartwright, a lineman on the team. He was a short, tough guy and we had a lot of fun together. We took trips to Dallas with some of the other guys on the team, which the coaches did not like. A few of my teammates were thought to be "thugs" by the coaching staff, and although they were on the team, the coaches didn't want me hanging out with them.

We had a little guard named George Dearborn, who was about a foot too short to play football. He looked like a little bowling ball knocking guys over on the field, and when we ran sweeps with both guards pulling, George would flatten anything in front of him. It's too bad he didn't have the physical makeup for pro ball, because he had what it took on the inside.

There was one guy on the team who came out of the army, Johnny Younger, but he wasn't that good. He used to run a Jimmy-game—like they called it at the time—and he'd get freshmen to play for 25 cents a pop, which was a lot of money to us. He might get me or somebody else to start the game and eventually end up with all of the freshmen's money—every dime of it. Younger was 10 years older than all of us, and I learned a lot from him. Was he a "thug?" No, but like a lot of the guys on the team, the coaches didn't like him, either.

I never understood why there would be players on the team whom the coaches didn't care for, especially when they were on scholarship.

The Homecoming game was always very special-a great event at the school. The alumni would come back, drink whiskey and party their heads off the whole weekend. There was always a parade that circled around the campus and a big party the Friday night before the game. We always heard partying and fun, but we couldn't leave our rooms the night before the game. I know some of the guys slipped out, but I never thought it was worth getting caught.

When the team walked from the dorm to the playing field, it was almost a straight shot through the campus. I would usually walk over with my little group, Cartwright, Buddy Gibson and the guys from Dallas, and the girls would holler "Have a good game" and wave as we went by. It took about twenty minutes to walk over there, because we always walked slower when we passed the girls' dorm.

We had big crowds for every game, and most of them were played at Blackshear Field, our home stadium. Blackshear Field was just that, a historic field, and it was almost like playing in a valley with a football field on it. Fans would have to sit on the hill that surrounded the field because the stands weren't very big back then. But despite those conditions, we were still very successful.

"My relationship with Otis is unique. We played together in the same conference—he was at Prairie View, and I was at Jackson State. We both played the same position—wide receiver. And he was an All-American at Prairie View. In fact, he was one of my idols. Otis was a guy everyone really looked up to because of his performance as an athlete on the field. I tried to duplicate that, and we fortunately ended up as teammates in the pros."

—Gloster Richardson, Chiefs Wide Receiver, 1967-70

I inspect my helmet as I prepare for a game at Prairie View. Jim Kearney, in the background, was our quarterback, and he was very good. He ended up playing safety in the pros and was also my teammate in Kansas City. He should have been a quarterback in the pros, too. (Photo courtesy of the Taylor Family Collection)

Since I'd been a quarterback in high school, I wanted to be one at Prairie View, and was, in fact, recruited to be a signal caller. But when I saw Jim Kearney throwing a ball 75 yards one day before practice, I knew I couldn't beat him out. Jim was a super quarterback, and even though he later had a very good career with the Chiefs as a defensive safety, he would have been a great pro quarterback. It was absolutely horrible that he wasn't given the chance because of the color of his skin. But pro football still wasn't ready for a black quarterback in the early 1960s, so Jim, along with numerous other players from the SWAC, was cheated out of an opportunity he would have had if he was white.

Since Kearney was a stellar quarterback, I asked the coach if I could change positions. Wide receiver was the natural choice, and I'm glad I made the move. Kearney and I ended up being quite the quarterback-receiver tandem throughout my career at Prairie View, and by my senior season we were virtually unstoppable. Here's an example from one of our better games: When we whomped Southern 60-14 in 1964, Jim ran the ball in twice for touchdowns and hit me three times for scores—the longest one from 62 yards out. We were undefeated national champs in 1963 and repeated in 1964 with a 10-1 record. I was given the honor of being team captain my senior season.

I had a few injuries during my time at Prairie View—the same ones I had in high school. When you get a knee injury it can be swollen for as long as three weeks and then all of a sudden it just stops. But—and this important to remember—if you were able to walk, you played. Pulled muscles, sprained knees, sore necks, it didn't matter...you played. With only 35-40 guys on the team—the bottom ten players weren't on scholarship—you had to play hurt. If you didn't play, you might lose your position and never get it back.

Some time after the start of my senior season, Lloyd Wells started coming to campus more and more, bringing pro football scouts with him to watch our practices. They were looking at five to eight guys on the team, and I was one of them. Mr. Wells and the other scouts would walk around the field and talk to us about our future plans. I had a feeling I could play pro ball, but I didn't know if I would be given a chance since I was at such a small school. I had seen a couple of Houston Oilers games and tried to do some small comparisons. From the beginning, Lloyd was very positive about my making it in the pros, but he said it was all up to me.

4

THE BABYSITTING CAPER

The story of how I ended up playing for the Kansas City Chiefs has become one of the great legends of pro football. The event—my choosing the American Football League over the National Football League—is looked upon by many of the sport's historians as one of the defining moments of the great money war that took place between the two leagues in the mid-1960s. And maybe it is, because it's a story that has everything: money, betrayal, intrigue and sex—real cloak and dagger stuff. It's a tale that's been told many, many times in the past 39 years. But a lot of legends, while holding small smatterings of reality and fact, are usually not entirely true.

This story is no exception.

As my senior season at Prairie View wound down, several pro teams from both the AFL and NFL made it known that they were interested in me. The injury to my knee was a bit of a concern, however—nobody wanted to invest in damaged goods—and as a result, my overall pre-draft value dropped a little. But heading into the 1964 Thanksgiving Day weekend, my spot in the draft didn't matter much to me, because by that time I was convinced I'd sign with the Kansas City Chiefs. Sportswriter and friend Lloyd Wells, who helped me choose Prairie View, took an active interest in where I'd play professional football. Lloyd was a part-time scout for the Chiefs and graded the talent at small black colleges in the south and southwest. Because of our long-term friendship, he convinced me that Kansas City was the place for me. I trusted his judgment.

The Chiefs had played in Houston the Sunday before Thanksgiving, and I was invited to the game. After meeting with Lloyd and some of the Chiefs executives, I figured that was it—Kansas City wanted me, and because of The Judge, I wanted them, too.

The best way to explain Lloyd Wells is to say he's an extravagant extrovert. When he's around, you know it. Always the center of attention, Lloyd was a ladies' man—by his own admission—and also crazy about sports and athletes. One thing, more than anything else about Lloyd that has always stuck with me, is that if something was said—plans were made or promises pledged—he made it happen and always followed through. That's the kind of guy he is. And maybe that's why his involvement in my signing might seem remarkable to some, but to me it was just standard operating procedure for Lloyd Wells.

As a scout, Lloyd worked directly for Chiefs head coach Hank Stram, which was a good thing, because he wasn't that popular within the rest of the organization—something I never understood. But Hank liked him, and that was lucky for the Chiefs because Lloyd was responsible for bringing a lot of talented African-Americans players to the team. The Judge was eventually rewarded for his scouting prowess and made a full-time scout for the team a couple of years after I became a Chief.

> *"I first saw him in junior high school and then at Worthing High School in Houston. As a young boy, about 15 or so, he was playing with the varsity—boys 18 and 19 years old. Otis was such a great talent. He played all sports—football, basketball, baseball and track."*
>
> —Lloyd Wells

Lloyd "The Judge" Wells, at the podium, dropping a few jokes on the crowd at a dinner in my honor in 1967. Lloyd made sure I became a Kansas City Chief. (Photo courtesy of the Taylor Family Collection)

Since it began play in 1960, the AFL's franchises had steadily increased their pursuit of the top players coming out of the college ranks. When ABC doled out 36 million dollars to the league for exclusive TV rights in 1963, the league had the new money—muscle it needed, and more money—a lot more money—spoke loudly to graduating football players. This resulted in a recruitment war with the NFL, and nothing was held back by either league. Contracts were thrust into the faces of players literally as they walked off the field following their final collegiate game. Others were wined and dined, then offered incredible sums of money (by the standard of the day) to sign. Inevitably, both leagues exaggerated the facts—truths, half-truths and outright lies—to get what they wanted. But lies or not, money seemed to talk the loudest. Joe Willie Namath of Alabama, one of the most coveted players in the class of 1965, selected the AFL's New York Jets over the NFL's St. Louis Cardinals, signing for a then-record $427,000.

The NFL had always used a standard ploy of pointing out the "inferiority" of the AFL to prospective players; it was the "Mickey Mouse" league. The best football was played in the NFL, or so we were told. The AFL's recruitment pitch offered a more positive view of the football world—giving its players a chance to become a part of a history-making new league. In the end, at least for me, it came down to the people I knew I'd be working with and playing for, which was one area where Kansas City had most teams—in both leagues—beaten hands down, at least as far as I was concerned.

> *"Lloyd Wells was working for us at that particular time, and he was an excellent scout. So we saw a lot of Otis and he was just very, very special. The first time I saw him catch the ball, I got butterflies—so soft, so easy. He was able to make the moves and the big plays. And he was smart, too. He made adjustments."*
>
> —Hank Stram

Following my weekend with the Chiefs in Houston, a representative of the Dallas Cowboys invited me—on behalf of the NFL—to spend Thanksgiving weekend in the Big D. It was a regional "party" for the top recruits in the area, and since the Cowboys, as well as the Philadelphia Eagles, had hopes of drafting and signing me, I was invited. It's always nice to be wanted, so I figured what the hell and decided to go. And this is where the story really begins—a tale that is probably more Lloyd Wells's than mine.

"Did Lloyd give Mother $100 bribe money? No, that's not true. I know better. My mother would have probably thrown it in his face or if he had sent it to her, she would have sent it back to him. Sometime during that weekend Lloyd called our house—it seemed like he was trying to throw someone off. I think when he called, my mother got really upset because Otis was supposed to be there to sign with the Cowboys. But Lloyd had always been like a mentor and Otis had been around him a lot. Lloyd thought highly of Otis—he would write in his columns about how good Otis was playing football. I don't know if Mother really wanted him to go to Kansas City, but after she didn't know where Otis was and found out that he was with Wells, she was kind of relieved about the whole thing."

—Florence Odell Taylor

The day before Thanksgiving, Seth Cartwright and I headed north from Prairie View to Dallas for the party, joining several other college players as the NFL's guests. The mix of players included a couple of guys from North Texas, one from the University of Kansas, and one from West Texas State. Altogether, there must have been about eight or nine college players there. What I didn't know—didn't even consider—was that the gathering was actually an NFL tactic to keep me and the others away from the AFL. The plan was simple—the Cowboys would keep me "hidden" until after the AFL's draft that upcoming Saturday, and then they would sign me to an NFL contract instead.

While I was on my way to Dallas, Wells was traveling to Nashville to pick up Gloster Richardson and bring him back to Kansas City with another player. After arriving in the Music City, he received a call from Lamar Hunt's secretary that I had left Prairie View and was on the way to Dallas. Remember, I had pretty much convinced Lloyd and the Chiefs that I was going to go with them. Still, he did the natural thing considering the combative, warlike climate that existed between the two leagues: He panicked.

Lloyd's a quick thinker, though, and after begging Gloster and the other player to stay put in Nashville, he immediately flew to Dallas and started his quest to find me. His plan of attack was simple: Check the hotels where it was believed the group of college players were staying—the Hilton, Sheraton and Executive—find me and take me back to Kansas City to sign a contract.

What was I doing as Lloyd began combing Dallas hotels? Not much. Over the course of three days we changed hotels three times, partied a little, watched a lot of TV, but generally just tried to overcome boredom. It felt like I was totally isolated from the rest of the world. If I had known the long weekend was going to be nothing more than a babysitting venture—where I was the baby—I would never have gone to Dallas. But it was exciting to be wanted, and I stayed because I wanted to stay. And when the Cowboys talked about teaming me with Bob Hayes, the world's fastest human at the time and another prominent recruit in the player signing war that year, I was thrilled. Maybe I was feeling impulsive, or just a little immature. Whatever it was—Lloyd Wells and the Chiefs notwithstanding—I was strongly considering the option of making the Cowboys or Eagles my team.

"Lloyd Wells was great when you asked him about somebody. I'd say, "Hey, go to so-and-so and take a look at this kid and see what you think." He'd come back and if he liked him, he'd say 'Out of sight.'

Everybody was out of sight. If he didn't like him, he'd say, 'I'll tell you what, Coach. I think the guy would be great selling programs at a football game.' Lloyd was terrific—a lot of fun, but serious about his work. And he got a lot of talent for us."

—Hank Stram

For three days Lloyd hunted for me, checking the hotel registers, talking with every Dallas contact he had. But the NFL was always a step ahead, moving us every day to a different location. On verge of giving up, The Judge finally made a few calls to Prairie View and then to my mom's house in Houston. It's at this point, however, where the story has several variations; I think Lloyd pulled a Dizzy Dean on several writers (telling a different version to everyone he talked with).

I'll sort the facts from the fiction.

Lloyd did call some of my friends at Prairie View, but I really don't know what information, if any, he got from them. When he called our house in Houston, it was my sister, not my mother, who answered the phone. Did my mother talk to him? I don't know. Lloyd also claimed to have "bribed" Mom with $100 for my whereabouts. It's not true. But regardless of those trivial differences in the story, he found out from my family the name of the girl in Dallas I had talked to. I have also read another version of this story that has Lloyd calling a friend at Prairie View who gave him a list of the girls I knew in Dallas large enough to fill a phone book. Ridiculous. The list wasn't more than ten names long. I guess this is where the sex thing supposedly comes into the story. Sorry to disappoint, but nothing like that happened.

I want to reiterate at this point that I was not "locked up" or being kept against my will in Dallas by the NFL. It was my choice to stay, and I could have left whenever I wanted. And I wasn't upset about the experience; mixed up, yes, but I was never mad. I left the watchful eye of the NFL reps just once; I had dinner with the girl who would eventually tell Lloyd where I was.

Some accounts of this "caper" claimed Lloyd was "posing" as a newspaperman to gain access to me at the motel. Lloyd was a newspaperman! And one way or another, most versions have the hotels crawling with plainclothesmen police, NFL security guards, and other personnel from the Cowboys. To this I can only say that I was watched, the NFL guys were conscious of keeping me away from anyone and everyone, and even my phone calls were monitored.

> *"Otis didn't work hard like the guys without the talent. He had natural talent, and it was obvious to everybody. He's the best wide receiver I've seen in high school, college or the pros. I'd put him up with anyone you can name."*
>
> —Lloyd Wells

Once Lloyd knew who the girl was that I had had contact with in Dallas, he called her and found out that I was at the Continental Motel in Richardson, Texas. Leaving no motor law unbroken, Lloyd allegedly made it in record time to the motel. Dodging the many NFL reps that seemed to be surrounding the place, he slipped $20 to a porter and asked if he knew where I was. Told we were possibly in a room by the pool—which we were—Lloyd picked out a door and knocked. It was the right room.

"I'm from *Ebony* magazine," Lloyd told one our watchers who answered the door. "I want to do a story on Otis Taylor." He presented one of his numerous press cards and was let in.

"Man, you're doing me wrong," Lloyd said when he finally laid eyes on me and we had the chance to talk somewhat privately. "We've been friends too long to let something like this happen."

He was right.

"Your mother is worried about you," he continued, "and she wants you to come with me. Don't worry, I'll fix everything." Part of his "fix" included a new red T-Bird, courtesy of the Chiefs. "Let's get out of here now."

> *"That was really something, the Dallas situation. I know bits and pieces about it. I know Otis was there and that he was going to sign with the Cowboys. I know Mother was getting nervous—it was something about Lloyd Wells wanting him to play with the Chiefs. I don't know whether Otis wanted to or he was talked into it, but one way or another, they sneaked him out of a window of a hotel."*
>
> —Florence Odell Taylor

But I didn't leave then, and I don't know why. I was young and mixed up, and while I knew what I wanted to do, it just took me a while to finalize my decision. I told Lloyd to come back later. After more encounters with the endless number of security guards milling about the motel, Lloyd returned in the evening. Seth's girlfriend was with us then, and she answered the door when he knocked and told him we still couldn't leave yet. He gave her his phone number at the Sheraton.

"Have Otis call me when he's ready to go." Lloyd returned to the Sheraton and waited anxiously to hear from me.

I finally called him at three o'clock in the morning, and Lloyd was there to pick me up by 3:30 a.m. As a final footnote for the caper—and one of the most famous moments of the entire episode—I climbed out of the motel window when I left the room; the front door was still guarded by the NFL's babysitting custodian. Lloyd drove us to the Fort Worth airport—he didn't think it would be safe at the Dallas airport—and we flew to Kansas City.

"I should have stayed with Otis, but I had known him for so long I thought he was safe. But I can understand how Otis felt. They picked him up in a cab and gave him all that attention. Any young kid would have been impressed."

—Lloyd Wells

There was snow on the ground in Kansas City, and strange as it seems, I'd never seen snow before in my life. And it was cold. Lloyd took me to Michaels, a men's clothing store in KC, and bought me a sweater, then checked me in at the Muehlbach Hotel. After that we went to the Chiefs' offices and met with Coach Stram, Lamar Hunt and Don Klosterman, the Chiefs' top scout, to work out the details of my contract. Later that day the Chiefs made it official and drafted me in the fourth round.

The details of my first professional contract were pretty good: a $15,000 salary, a $15,000 signing bonus, and the best part, as far as I was concerned, a beautiful red T-Bird. The total package was worth around $45,000 when all the incidentals and extras were added together. I was happy and the Chiefs were happy. I think Lloyd was just relieved that I hadn't gotten away from him.

When I finally signed that first contract with the Chiefs, the excitement I felt was almost beyond words. It wasn't just the money, which was more than I ever dreamed of at the time, or the team, which had proved more than any other that it really wanted me, or even the new car. My excitement had a lot to do with the situation I grew up in, basically having nothing financially my entire life, and I now had the opportunity to be a success not just for myself, but for my mother, sister and dad—for the love of my family.

"Otis and I were in the same conference when we were in college. He was at Prairie View and I was at Southern, and we had been dueling

the whole time. He got drafted by Kansas City in the fourth round, and I was also drafted by Kansas City in the fourth round—he was 4A and I was 4B. They also brought in Gloster Richardson, who was from Jackson State, so we all came to Kansas City together, and we were all out of the Southwestern Athletic Conference."

—Frank Pitts, Chiefs Wide Receiver, 1965-70

That 1965 AFL draft turned out to be a pretty good one for the Chiefs. After selecting me, they drafted Frank Pitts with their second fourth-round selection, and then they grabbed Gloster Richardson—one of the guys under Lloyd's watchful eye in Nashville—and the three of us, all receivers, played together in Kansas City through the end of the decade. As good a group of draft selections as Frank, Gloster and I were, it could have been a lot better. The University of Kansas's Gayle Sayers, who would become one of the greatest running backs in the history of the NFL, was the team's top draft choice. He snubbed the Chiefs, though, and opted for the NFL's Chicago Bears. Linebacker Mike Curtis of Duke was selected just before me in the third round, and he slipped through the team's fingers also, signing instead with the Baltimore Colts.

Thus ended my "babysitting" caper. I knew at the time it was an unusual sequence of events, but never did I imagine I'd retell the tale so many times and for so many years.

"All I know is that it was mighty cloak and dagger," Lloyd said of his most famous scouting escapade. "That's how I'd describe it."

5

GOIN' TO KANSAS CITY

I'd like to say my confidence was sky high when I left Houston for my first training camp with the Kansas City Chiefs in the summer of 1965. I'd also like to say that I knew exactly what to expect and that I was ready to impress the Chiefs with my talent and athletic ability. I did have confidence, but what I remember more than anything else was being scared—really scared.

I did not want to fail.

I loaded everything I owned into my new red T-Bird and made the long drive from Houston to Kansas City. I thought about the upcoming challenges I would face playing pro football on the drive and tried to prepare myself mentally. Fear of failure can be a great motivator, especially if you don't have an alternative plan lined up. Without football, I have no idea what I would have done.

As it turned out, my rookie season with the Chiefs was a very testing year. I was far from home for the first time in my life, and I wasn't the star of the team for the first time ever—I wasn't even a starter until the final three games. I had to learn about pro football, but more importantly, I needed to learn about Kansas City—the place—and where I could and could not go. There were specific regions of the city—bars, restaurants, stores—that we were warned to stay away from. And when I say we, I mean the African-American players. We also got briefings from the AFL's front office on how to conduct ourselves. In every city we played in we were warned and given suggestions on how to behave, a policy that seems very out-of-date today. It was quite an adjustment.

"Otis and I had a great time in Kansas City. What was so great about it was that we were both single guys at the time. And with him being a star, and me being a guy on the team, I got some of the action without even trying."

—Gloster Richardson

There was a bowling alley that we went to at 43rd and Indiana in Kansas City—the only bowling alley in town where we were allowed in. It was a fun spot. People bowled and there was a bar—I must admit I spent a lot of hours in that bar—and I made friends with a lot of Chiefs fans. At that time, the team meant so much to the community—the whole organization was very important to the town. But our choices of where to go were really limited when it came to the "white" part of town.

African Americans weren't really allowed on the Country Club Plaza. There was a saying in the black community: "You get your ass off the Plaza before six." However, most of the segregated areas in town didn't stop the African-American Chiefs players from eating or shopping in their establishments. When they found out the black men were football players, they accepted us and our money. This sounds rotten, and I suppose it was, but by letting us in, they eventually let all blacks in. I've gotten mad at some of the church and organization leaders in Kansas City through the years for not giving the

A posed shot for the press. I'm showing off my record collection in Kansas City. Marvin Gaye was always my favorite. (Photo provided by AP/WWP)

Chiefs players any thanks for what we did when things were tough in the city for minorities. And I think we did a lot.

But '65 was also a good year. I was learning what it meant to really be out on my own and do things for myself. Gloster Richardson and I were roommates, and we lived across from Satchel Paige Ballpark—right off Swope Park. The apartments we lived in were considered luxury apartments in those days and are still up-to-date today. I met so many great people who had an interest in sports that first year in Kansas City. I had a very good friend—actually almost a second mother—in Maxine Byrd. She had a restaurant and I started eating there in 1965 and continued to eat there until the place had to close a couple of years ago. She was very traditional and had great food.

> *"Kansas City was a redneck, prejudiced town in 1965. The famous streets of 18th and Vine were still happening. The black clubs, the black music was all on Vine Street. Main Street was the white side and it was just an unspoken thing—if you were black you didn't go there. But I wasn't that kind of guy. I came from a different environment. You can't direct me on where to go and where not to go. I naturally gravitate toward places I'm not supposed to be. So KC was a town that just needed to be awakened. My problem was trying to get the black guys on the team to come and associate on the side of town that I went to, but none of them would ever go. They all went to Gates Bar-B-Q—that's where they hung out. It was a nightclub and also a restaurant that had ribs. It was okay for a while, but life and the world have got to be bigger than Gates Bar-B-Q."*
>
> —Fred Williamson

That first training camp I went through with the Chiefs was difficult. Coach Stram established who the boss was; he never wanted

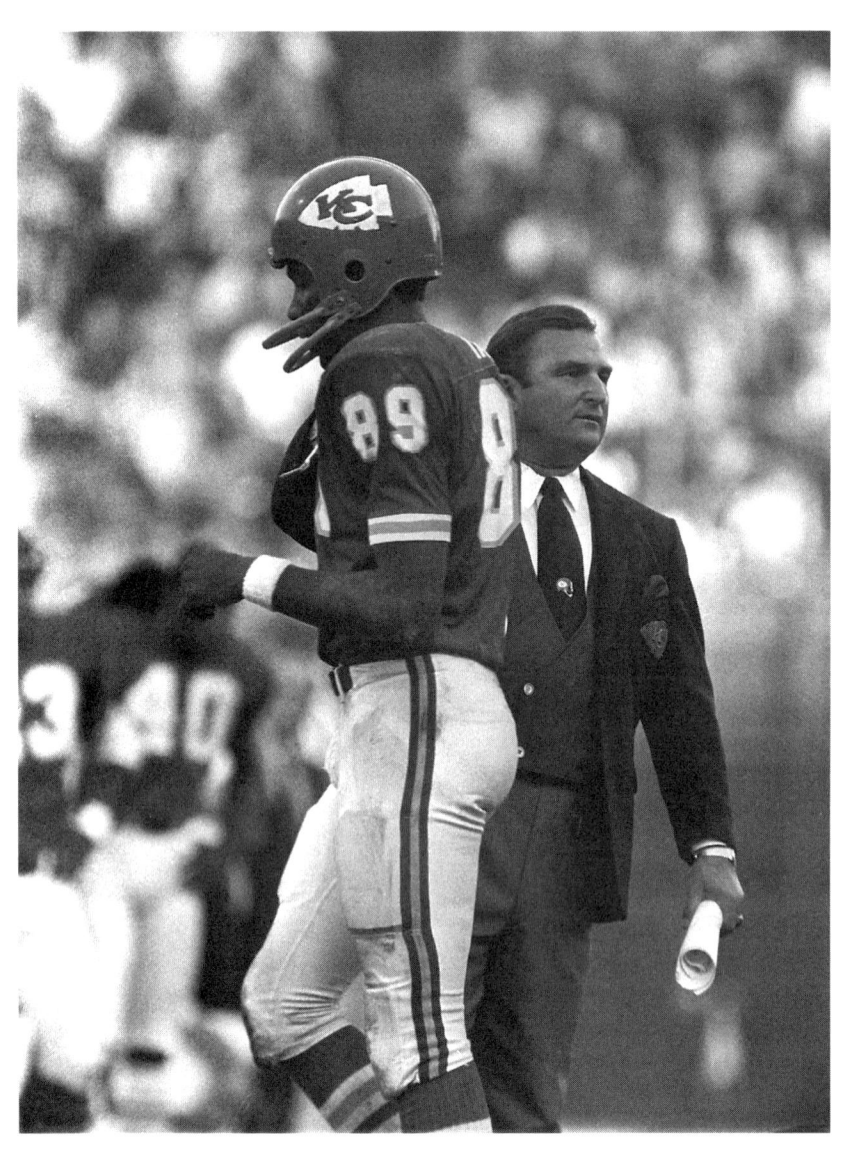

Congratulations from Hank Stram—the coach you loved and hated, but always respected. (Photo provided by the Kansas Collection, U. of Kansas Archives)

anyone to doubt for a second that he was in charge. It was foreign to me, being at the first camp. I know a lot of rookies who go to their first camp thinking they've got it made. I remained scared of not making the team right up to the final cut.

On top of the regular pressure of just trying to make the team, we had to endure the rookie "ritual" junk the Chiefs' veterans put on us. It was mostly good-natured stuff—a test of your mind and willingness to be embarrassed more than anything else. One of the standard tests took place as we ate our team meals. Each rookie would be called up to the front of the room by one of the veteran players and told to sing his school song. I made up my mind to go along and have fun.

"Otis, get up here and put your hand on your heart." I got up, moved to the front and put my hand on my heart. No big deal.

"Not that heart, your other heart!" and the player—Buck Buchanan—motioned to my crotch. Everyone was laughing. I said okay and grabbed my groin.

"Now sing your school song." So I filled the cafeteria with my beautiful voice and the lyrics of Prairie View's alma mater:

> *Dear Prairie View, our song to thee we raise.*
> *In gratitude, we sing our hymn of praise.*
> *For memories dear, for friends and recollections,*
> *For lessons learned while here we've lived with thee.*
> *For these we pledge our hearts...*

I was laughing by the end of the song, enjoying the moment, and the rest of the guys were laughing, too. Maybe I was a little off key.

The greatest part of what I learned during that first training camp about the embarrassing stuff pulled on rookies was that it was a test. The small hazing things were done for a reason. The established players and coaches wanted to see how you'd react and if you'd mesh and blend with the team's camaraderie. Throughout my eleven years of playing, I saw rookies say they weren't going to do it and wouldn't do anything. And those players didn't stay around very long—they got rid of them fast. The coaches, as well as the players, were looking for tough, talented players who would follow instructions and conform to the team atmosphere.

> *"Any time I talk about Otis Taylor, I feel like I'm talking about the greatest. As a receiver, he was one of the toughest hard-nosed players in the game. The thing I remember about Otis, wherever he was flanked, I knew if I had the ball, I could count on him coming across to block and I could make my cut. I could see it before it even happened because he was just that dependable. I think the guy really loved blocking as much as he did catching—I know he did. I smelled him, saw him, looked him in the eye in the huddle, and knew he'd be there."*
>
> —Curtis McClinton, Chiefs Running Back, 1962-69

Throughout my years as an athlete I acquired several nicknames, a lot of them that first year in Kansas City: Big O (the same as basketball great Oscar Robertson, but probably my favorite, and one I'd had since high school), Slug, T-Bag, Hefty T-Bag, O. T., and Big Head. I was called Big O and O. T. more than the others. Big Head was literally because of my big head. I always had to have a specially sized helmet, and sometimes that caused problems. I never did figure out where the T-Bag name came from, and Slug was from a fight that never really happened.

I had a great receivers coach, Pete Brewster. He was very patient and gave me a lot of confidence—the confidence I initially lacked when I first joined the team. A lot of my skills were developed under Pete's tutelage. During the course of my career, he worked us hard. Of

I scored on this play, but had to be helped from the field after crashing into the embankment wall at Municipal Stadium in Kansas City. Mike Garrett is at the far left in the photo. (Photo courtesy of the Taylor Family Collection)

all the players, Chris Burford, the first great receiver to play for the Chiefs, was my mentor. Burford was slow, and it sometimes seemed like he ran in slow motion. But he could run a pattern—he ran six-yard out patterns perfectly every time. I learned a lot from just watching him play. Frank Jackson was the other receiver, and he was also very good. I played on the side that Jackson was on about half of the season. I wasn't starting, but I didn't have to start because after a couple of minutes I usually got into the game and played a lot.

I didn't have blocking skills to speak of that first year, either. The only time I blocked at Prairie View was if someone got in the way. I was usually bigger and knocked them down. But if you played offense for the Chiefs, you blocked. I learned how to crack back on the linebacker—you hit them above the waist. I always made sure they knew they were hit, too.

I also didn't really know how to run a pass pattern when I left Prairie View because it wasn't necessary. Jim Kearney just told us where to run. We'd just go, and he'd throw. We scored 40-50 touchdowns every year, so why would we need to run patterns? When I came to the Chiefs, I found they did things on a more precise level—organized, planned and detailed. For example, they did a six-yard out because the guy on the inside was doing a 13-yard curl, and the guy on the outside of him is doing a post pattern. All that means something, and I had to learn what it meant and do it. Basically, it meant you were freeing up somebody else or freeing up yourself. Chris taught me how to run patterns. He knew that sooner or later I'd take his job, and he was a hell of a man about it. That's what he was. He, of all people, tried to help. So I was pretty lucky that first season.

Following the next to last game of the 1965 season, Mack Lee Hill, the Chiefs' best running back, died during routine knee surgery. Mack was only about 5'10" or 5'11" tall, and he weighed 225-235 pounds. He had a big build, was strong as an ox, and had a high, squeaky voice that accompanied the permanent smile on his face. Everything he did was with a smile. This might sound a little funny, but I can still feel some of Mack Lee's actions—his warm effect on me.

Mack was so joyful on the football field the way he ran over or through would-be tacklers. He had a tremendous fire within his heart and was a special person to our ball club. It shocked us immensely when he died. Why such a horrible tragedy happened to somebody like Mack Lee Hill is a question that sticks in your mind forever.

"We seemed a little snake-bit there because we had a couple players that died within a three-year span, and that gets a little scary. Now, Mack passed away on the operating table getting a simple knee op-

eration and for a number of different reasons why, and they all were speculation. I had surgery with the same physician involved about a month before on my shoulder. My shoulder kind of came apart on me when I was out in L.A. I was driving back and going up to the Bay area because I didn't know if I was going to be able to play any more. I had a really bad separation—ligament damage in the shoulder. And I had a couple of pins put in, and the pins started working their way out when I was driving back. So I had to have it operated on when I got to the Bay area. It was not good. That's why I didn't know if I was even going to play any more after that injury. It worked out and I was able to play. The Mack Lee Hill thing, I was gone when that happened. I really read about it and talked to people about it on the telephone because I was out on the West Coast when it happened. That was a tremendous shock to the team, too. You can do a lot of things, but you don't expect to die from them when you're playing."

—Chris Burford, Chiefs Wide Receiver, 1960-67

Mack has been on everyone's mind—his teammates, coaches and friends—since the day it happened. We all had a great deal of respect for him, not just for the kind of football player he was, but for the kind of human being he was. Mack Lee put a lot of faith and high standards into a lot people's lives for a short period of time. The Chiefs honored him, starting in 1966 (the following season), by naming the team's Rookie of the Year award after him. The award is presented to the player who shows the type of hustle, love and respect for teamwork that Mack played with more than any of his other physical attributes—the player with the most heart.

The team dedicated the final game of the 1965 season to Mack, and there was only one other game I played in for the Chiefs that was filled with that much passion. That was against the Bears in 1967. We played a little sloppy, with way too much emotion, but still beat the Broncos 45-35. The Chiefs finished with a 7-5-2 record in 1965, and personally, I accomplished a lot. Although I only caught 26 passes, I averaged more than 17 yards per catch and scored five touchdowns. I was truly a professional football player, and I knew good things were in my future.

When the season ended I went back to Prairie View and took a couple of classes. I was still short some hours to finish my degree, but I didn't make things too hard because I wasn't in any big rush. I had an apartment off campus, visited my family a lot in Houston and took some trips to Dallas in my Thunderbird.

"I really had picked up a little bit as a receiver in five seasons. Otis was just coming out of college, and while it was competitive, we always tried to help the other receivers. You never minded helping somebody who you knew was going to help the ball club, who was going to be a good player. Otis always wanted to learn, and he didn't mind me telling him something now and then that I thought might be helpful to him. We did play the same position. When he first came in, he played right behind me as a wide out primarily on the left side. And on the other side, I think Frank Jackson was over there, and Gloster, and I think Frank Pitts kind of floated back and forth between the two positions. I got hurt in 1965 in November. I tore up my shoulder back in Boston against the Patriots, and then Otis stepped in and started in my spot the last three games. So the next season, I didn't know if I was going to be able to come back or not. They moved to Otis to the right side and traded Frank Jackson off to Miami, I believe. So then, Otis and I were both starting."

—Chris Burford

•••

THE NEED TO WIN

Gloster Richardson, in the sunglasses, and me. Note the Chiefs crest on the jackets, one of Coach Stram's mandatory dress items when we traveled. (Photo courtesy of the Taylor Family Collection)

"He could break the game wide open with one catch. In any given game, Otis could make a catch that would turn the game completely around. Things might be going against us, and then the next thing you know, BANGO, a big play. He consistently did that in every game. And you need that on the offense. As a team, you look for people who can make these plays. You can be chugging along in the game, and it could be even-up, but you know it's just a matter of time before someone would break things open. And that's what Otis did-break things open."

—Bobby Bell

When I first met Chiefs head coach Hank Stram, he was what I would call "smooth and fluid." After my second year with the club he was just fluid, and by my third season with him he was Hank. But all along, he was always the coach we loved to hate. You loved him, but you hated him. Hank was a ruler—his way or no way, and we all understood that. Coach Stram was a great coach, and I'm really delighted he's been inducted into the Pro Football Hall of Fame. He was a real winner.

Hank was a coach who was very protective of his players—from the media especially—but he also liked being in the limelight. Before each game he was always a little nervous in the locker room and never really made what you would call a dramatic speech before we went out to the field. He usually stood in the middle of the room and told us what we needed to do to win and exactly what he expected of us. I also liked him because he liked clothes as much as I do and always wanted to look his best. When we traveled to another city for a game, the rule was to get there by Saturday afternoon for a Sunday afternoon game—24 hours before kickoff. He would take four or five suits with him, even though we were only going to be gone for a day and a half. But he had to have extra suits if he wanted to talk to the press Saturday night, and on Sunday morning he would go to church. He had a blazer that he wore for the game. Hank would change many times over the weekend, depending on how long we were going to be in town. He never did like to wear anything twice. I remember watching his wife struggle as she carried three pieces of luggage to the plane as we were boarding, and he'd be carrying only one bag. The players used to help her out, and maybe that's what Hank wanted in the first place.

Coach Stram's practice demeanor could be pretty tough. When we went through our warmup routines at the start of practice, Hank wanted everyone to be in full gear—helmet on, shoulder pads, everything. If anybody took something off, a pad or something, he knew, and he would get really pissed. At times I know his shit list had to be pretty long. I would end up on that shit list at least three times every season, usually for dumb stuff. And it was always hard to get off the list, once you were one it. Hank always saw everything that everyone did because he watched most of the practices from his "cherry picker," one of those rising buckets that are similar to what the phone company uses to fix problem wires.

There was a particular practice session and sequence of events in the early 1970s that sums up my overall relationship with Coach Stram. I was running down the sidelines catching balls from Mike Livingston, one of our quarterbacks. He started throwing deep passes, and I started trying to catch the ball behind my back with one hand. You never know when you'll need to catch a ball like that in a game situation, so I liked to practice the one-handed catches every now and then. But after I caught a ball behind my back, Coach Stram, who was perched up in his cherry picker, started screaming at me.

"Damn it! Catch the ball right. Don't catch the ball like that behind you. Catch the ball in your hands in front of you."

"Come on, man," I said, "there might be an instance when I'll need to catch it like that." He yelled to stop again, so I started catching the balls in front of me. Then somebody asked, "Big O, you going to try it again?" and I said sure. So I ran up the field, turned sideways to catch the pass in the back with one hand. Initially I thought I missed the ball, but then I caught it on my right hip. That's when I heard Coach Stram again.

"Damn it, I told you to catch the ball with your hands in front of you! That's $500!" He was still up in the cherry picker-he liked being 50 feet higher than anybody else. I walked right by the picker and left the field.

"Screw it," I said to no one in particular. "I'm tired of you messing with me." I was really pissed at him for picking on me, and I slammed my helmet down, breaking it. As I stormed off the field, I heard Hank yelling at Bobby Yarlborough, our equipment manager, who was driving the cherry picker.

"Let me down, Bobby, let me down." Bobby saw how upset I was, heard me swearing—I also said I was tired of everyone messing with me in the angriest of tones—and I'm sure everyone else on the field heard me, too. I was ready to hit someone, specifically Hawk.

"Coach, I think you ought to stay up there because Otis is mad. He's really mad." Coach Stram, so I was told later, thought for a second before speaking again. The picker was almost to the ground.

"Lift it back up there," Hank told Bobby. "Lift it back up." And so the picker went back up, and he let me go to the locker room. I showered and was getting ready to leave when I found out Hank wanted to see me in the morning. I went out and got a little drunk that night. A $500 fine was a lot in those days, and I was pretty sore about it.

I went to see Coach Stram the following morning. He had this glorious office upstairs at Arrowhead, with four desks, cabinets, bookcases and all that in it. Before I went up to see Hank, the guys in the dressing room wanted know: "What are you going to tell him, Big

O?" I said I was going to tell him to quit messing with me and that I wasn't going to take his crap any more.

"You tell him, Big O!"

I was ready for a major confrontation when I entered Coach Stram's office. In fact, I was so angry I wanted to slug him and quit the team.

"Otis, you're my man," Hank said when I walked in. "What's happening? Sit down, sit down. You want some coffee or donuts or something?" He had a soda on his desk. He always had to have some sweets around. Then he asked me if everything was all right, and I said everything wasn't too good. We exchanged a couple more meaningless words and then he said, "You know, you're just like me, you're just like a part of the family, just like a son," and he got up and grabbed me and gave me a hug.

"I'm not going to fine you," he said in a very somber tone. "But don't tell anyone.

"And Otis, I love you."

I told him I loved him, too, and I started to cry and so did he.

I left his office wiping my eyes and went back to the dressing room. When I walked in the door, everybody was waiting, wanting to know what happened. So I told them.

"I told [Coach Stram] to quit @#$%ing with me and that I wasn't going to take it no more." Everyone laughed, saying I was the man.

Hank Stram was a coach that you loved to hate, and also just plain loved. He was also a coach for whom I would do anything. I remember many occasions when we would be practicing and the Astroturf would be 110 degrees. We'd run several 100-yard dashes and when we got through with the last one, Coach Stram would say, "Hey boys, I got something for you." And the trainer would bring out a keg of beer and some ribs. So how could you hate him? I think

Coach Stram really enjoyed his ability to lead. He tried different things to see what would work in a leadership role. We had our little confusions, arguments and disagreements over the years, but I can truly say I am a better man because Hank was my coach.

> *"We felt strongly about the team. We were all about 'we.' We were all about 'us,' not about 'you,' not about 'me,' not about 'I.' It was the feeling we had. The greatest definition of that team—I'm trying to paint a picture as far as the loyalty in the team aspect of it—is that they were hard-working. They took an awful lot of pride in what they did and how they did it. The players took a lot of pride in the fact that they were on our football team. The discipline, the great attitude our team had and the feeling they had for each other, the camaraderie and all that kind of stuff—it was really interesting. We were one of the first teams that started mini-camp in 1967. We got the players jobs in the city and they were very, very close to Kansas City. They loved being in KC."*
>
> —Hank Stram

The white-black racial situation in Kansas City hadn't started to change very much in 1965. But thank God for guys like Sherrill Headrick. He didn't know anything about race and didn't care. Headrick was a tough and wild linebacker who played fearlessly. He also played routinely with injuries, and his reckless nature, coupled with an all-out disrespect for his body, earned him the nickname "Psycho" from his teammates. His overall talent was mostly from within—from the heart—and he was a fun guy. We all liked him, and I cared a lot about him. I still do, because he was that type of guy. He could pull you together. He used to love to go out with me and Gloster. We did shooters—with lemon and other stuff—and if you missed one you had to do three. Headrick was a mentor, at least when it came to partying. He was a wild man. Most importantly, he never cared what color anyone was, and that rubbed off on a lot of people.

Before each game, after we'd get through warming up on the field, we'd go back to the locker room 20-30 minutes before kickoff. Headrick set his personal clock to when the team would leave the field, and he'd go in a few minutes before everyone else. When the rest of the team came into the locker room, the smell would hit us square in the face like a brick to the forehead—right at the door, just like it was a bomb or something. Headrick would be sitting on the toilet throwing up from one end, and crapping from the other. You just had to cover your nose to keep from getting sick too. I never smelled anything else that bad in my life, but Headrick's routine had become customary for the team. If that didn't happen before the game, we weren't ready to play. If he didn't throw up, he said, he didn't feel right.

"I've gotten sick before every game I've played in since college," Headrick once said of his pregame ritual. "It's my nervous stomach."

He broke his finger during a game my first year. I was sitting on the bench at the time—a little sore because I wasn't playing much. Headrick came to the sideline and it looked like his finger was hanging by the skin. I couldn't believe it, and the trainer was slow getting there to help him. Sherrill yelled at the trainer put a couple of sticks on and tape it up, because he had to get back in the game. They taped it together and he ran back on the field. Just looking at the finger hanging there was too much for me. I almost passed out I was so scared. The things he did to his poor body. Sherrill Headrick was one tough son of a bitch on the football field.

"Chris Burford had a shoulder injury, and Otis came in toward the end of the year [1965] to take his place. When we came back the next year, I was still on the special team. As a matter of fact, they had tabbed me as 'board hands.' I had real bad hands and had problems

catching the ball. I just made up my mind that if I wanted to be a pro football player then I had to start catching the ball. I admired Otis because he was responsible for a lot of our success the next year. Len Dawson just went crazy with him after he learned that when Otis caught the ball he could turn it into a touchdown. Then I just stepped it up, too. I couldn't let him leave me behind. It was time for me to get on the horse and start riding."

—Frank Pitts

The Chiefs ripped through the AFL in 1966—no one ever really stopped us. The club traded away Frank Jackson, and I became the other starting wideout with Burford. We both had great seasons. I caught 58 passes for 1,297 yards and eight touchdowns; Burford also caught 58 passes for 758 yards and eight touchdowns. The offense scored more than 40 points four times and we finished with an 11-2-1 record and the Western Division championship. We lost to Oakland and Buffalo at home, but beat both of them handily on the road. Eleven Chiefs were named to the AFL All-Star team, including me for the first time.

We played the 1966 AFL championship game in Buffalo on New Year's Day, 1967. They had a crappy, old stadium. It was really run down with old wood bleachers, and it was too cold to play football that day. Lord have mercy, it was cold. Snow was packed up on the sideline maybe seven feet high. I had a good game—the whole team did, really—but all I remember is the cold weather. I scored our second touchdown on a quick post pattern from 29 yards out. I wasn't sure I would make the end zone because of the hit I took, but nothing was going to keep from going in for the score. I finished with five receptions for 78 yards. Our defense was super, holding the Bills to 255 total yards and collecting four turnovers.

The biggest play of the game came late in the first half when Johnny Robinson, our free safety, picked off a pass at the goal line

I'm hauling in a pass in the 1966 AFL championship game in wet and cold Buffalo. (Photo provided by **The Topeka C-J***).*

and returned it 72 yards to the Buffalo 28-yard line. Our kicker, Mike Mercer, booted a 32-yard field goal just before halftime to put us up 17-7. Mike Garrett scored a couple touchdowns in the second half and that was the game—Kansas City 31, Buffalo 7.

The funny thing about Buffalo and that game was that we couldn't leave right away because of the weather. We had to go back to the hotel. Lamar Hunt got us some sandwiches and a ballroom to wait in until things cleared up a little. The funniest thing about the whole day happened while we were waiting in the hotel. Lamar was sitting with his legs crossed, and the penny loafers he was wearing had holes in them. Bobby Bell said, "Lamar, look at that...you have holes in your shoes." Lamar didn't get flustered or embarrassed—remember he was worth millions then and today—and said, "I walked up and down a lot during the game. The press box here has old brick on the floor." We had supposedly scared him so much during that game that he paced and paced, wearing the holes into the soles of his shoes.

Anyway, Bobby had everyone dying with laughter over Lamar Hunt's shoes.

6

HAMMERED

We were the 1966 AFL champs and the first team to ever win any kind of major championship for Kansas City. More importantly, we would represent the league in the first-ever Super Bowl. We ran off the cold, wet, miserable field of Buffalo's War Memorial Stadium into the locker room and just went crazy. The shrieking, hollering, laughing, and spraying champagne everywhere and at everyone lasted for more than half an hour. Tony Di Pardo led the Chiefs' Zing-Band with a rendition of "California, Here I Come." We threw Coach Stram into the shower and doused Lamar Hunt with the bubbly. And Sherrill Headrick, our great warrior of a linebacker, perched himself on a trunk—wearing nothing but a hat and smile—took some big slugs from a bottle and announced to the room how happy he was. The AFL had a ridiculous rule against champagne in the locker room, and I heard the Chiefs were later fined $2,000 by the league. It didn't matter, because we weren't going to let stupid rules stop our well-deserved celebration.

When we finished going crazy in the locker room, we moved the party to the hotel (because of the bad weather) and celebrated for another hour before leaving for the airport. Once on the plane, we started again, and it was the best ride home I ever had. Our fans, more than 12,000 of them, were waiting for us at the Municipal Airport in Kansas City, but as we approached the city, the captain scared us a little, announcing we would have to circle until given the clearance to land. It seemed there were people all over the runway, and it would take a while to clear them away.

Kansas City was very, very happy that we were champs.

"We hit the champagne pretty heavily after the game in the dressing room. I think everyone was very elated—very up. I was looking forward so much to playing against Green Bay or anybody on the NFL side because we'd gotten so much verbal abuse in Sports Illustrated *and the national rags. Our preparation for the game, I felt, was good. When we went out on the field, I thought we were fresh—ready to go. We had some good things to utilize, some of which didn't get used much in the game just because of the nature in which the game developed. I felt very confident. I think everybody felt pretty confident going into that game. And then, we'd seen the films and we had as much team speed or more than they had in my mind—size-wise and everything else. They just had the big reputation."*

—Chris Burford

The Chiefs were going to face the Green Bay Packers in the AFL-NFL world championship game (Lamar Hunt called the game the Super Bowl, but it would still be a couple of years before that became the official name for the game), a team considered then and today to be one of the greatest ever assembled. They were coached by Vince Lombardi—still considered the greatest football coach of all time by many people.

By the time we got off the plane, the all-out media onslaught against the Chiefs and the AFL had begun. The Mickey Mouse League comments and inferior-play stuff were dredged up, especially by newspapers in NFL cities. It was initially reported that the Chiefs were eight-point underdogs, then 13, and even though NFL coaches Tom Landry of the Dallas Cowboys and George "Papa Bear" Halas of the Chicago Bears made gracious public statements saying that maybe the Chiefs could beat the Packers, nobody believed them.

"I think [the Chiefs] can play [Green Bay] a good game," Landry said when asked about Kansas City's chances. The Packers had held off a late charge by Landry's Cowboys to win the NFL title game, 34-27. "The Chiefs are the underdogs and nobody expects them to do well."

Halas talked about the AFL's emphasis on defense the past five seasons; in reality, the league was offense, offense, offense. Different player matchups were overanalyzed as they always are in big games, but this one had a new twist since it was the first time teams from the two leagues would meet on the football field. The feeling was universal, though, as to what the outcome of the game would be: Almost everyone felt the Chiefs would lose, and lose big.

Usually that kind of stuff didn't bother our team—or me—and anything negative written about us was ignored or used as inspiration. But it was different this time. Looking back on the events leading up that first Super Bowl, I don't think anyone on our team truly thought we could beat Green Bay, either.

"When we played the Green Bay Packers in the first championship game, we felt bad because we were in it the first half, 14-10, and then they pulled away. They beat the NFL teams worse than they beat us. They had a heck of a team—just like we had a heck of a team in 1969."

—Ed Budde

We flew to Los Angeles 11 days before the first-ever Super Bowl to begin our preparations in Long Beach, or maybe I should say the team flew on one flight, and I flew on another. Of all the stupid things I could have done, I missed the team plane and had to catch a later flight. The time just got away from me—I wasn't paying attention and overslept—and before I knew it, the plane was taking off without me. Of course Coach Stram fined me. Hell, I would have fined myself if it had been possible. The saving grace to my embarrassment was that we were still ten days out from the game, and I hoped the press would take it easy on me. I shouldn't have worried.

Fred "The Hammer" Williamson took the media spotlight almost as soon as we landed in Los Angeles, becoming a self-proclaimed Pied Piper because, as he said, "Wherever I would go, the media would follow me for a quote."

Fred "The Hammer" Williamson in 1966. (Photo provided by the Kansas City Chiefs)

They followed him in droves that first week we were training in Long Beach.

"I haven't seen anything in the films that offers much of a threat to me," Freddy, a cornerback, told the press in his usual braggadocio manner. He was talking about the Packers' passing game. "I'll be able to cover either Boyd Dowler or Carroll Dale." These weren't the kind of things you said about Packer players, but Freddy didn't care. "Dale and Dowler don't have the speed or the combination of moves of Otis Taylor." Okay, I liked that. But Freddy talked on and on. He talked about architecture (he was a licensed architect), one of his favorite subjects. He talked about how other AFL receivers—San Diego's Lance Allworth and Buffalo's Elbert Dubenion in particular—were better than anyone Green Bay had.

"I'll bump [Dowler] as he leaves the line of scrimmage. If he catches the ball, then I'll drop the hammer on him." Then he said he'd drop the hammer on the whole Packers team.

I'll say this: Freddy was one of the dirtiest players in either league. When a receiver caught a ball on him, he would invariably swing a forearm hard into the unfortunate guy's head and knock the piss out of him—a hard, dirty hit, or as Fred preferred to described it, "a blow delivered with great velocity perpendicular to the Earth's latitudes."

Fred scared the hell out of a lot of players just by lining up opposite them, which was the point, I guess. But was it necessary to tell the greatest team in the history of professional football that they better keep a supply of extra helmets at the game to replace the ones he was going to shatter?

Most of the Packers, when asked about Williamson, politely declined to say anything about his comments. But Jim Taylor, their big, hard-running fullback, couldn't stay quiet.

"When the whistle blows we'll confront him with the situation of being between a rock and a hard place," Taylor said of Williamson, "and we'll see which way he goes." The Packers, Taylor continued, would do their talking after the game.

As a team and to a man, we had planned on keeping our mouths shut to the press and showing nothing but reverence and respect for the Packers. Freddy's comments rocked the boat considerably and really pissed off most of Green Bay's players. It pissed off a lot of Chiefs, too.

The thing is, Freddy was just being Freddy.

The Hammer always had his own agenda. After he joined the Chiefs, me and few of the other guys on the team followed him to the Country Club Plaza—the top shopping and dining district in Kansas City—to eat and hang out. That was a place that wasn't exactly warm to the idea of entertaining African Americans when I first arrived in the city. But he'd been around the block more than once, and whatever he wanted to do, he did. Freddy also openly dated white women, which was taboo in those days. A former marine, karate expert and future movie star, he came to the Chiefs in a trade with Oakland for Dave Grayson. He had always been his own man. He was never one to conform to how others thought he should live his life, and a move to Kansas City wasn't going to make him change his lifestyle. Freddy even lived on the Plaza, which was unheard of for blacks at the time. Imagine The Hammer living in the predominately black neighborhood around 51st and Swope. Was the world crazy?

Unfortunately, a lot of the guys with the Chiefs didn't like Freddy. I liked and respected him, but I also told him that if he ever hit me with his goddamn hammer in practice I'd kick his ass. He never did drop it on me—didn't even try—but he did put some pretty good coverage on me.

The biggest Hammer bombshell before the championship game came when *Life* magazine published an article on Chiefs players' nicknames and quoted many of the things Freddy said he was going to do to the Packers. A lot of the white guys on the team were pissed, though, and felt he had shed a bad light on the Chiefs to a national audience. Johnny Robinson and Chris Burford made public statements to that effect. The black guys, on the other hand, didn't care and felt Fred had a right to say whatever he wanted.

"That was Fred's personality," Buck Buchanan said of the Hammer's many comments before the Super Bowl. "He had a lot of confidence…He was just doing his thing."

"I've cracked open 30 helmets with [the Hammer] since I've been in the pros. I grab the guy with one arm anywhere from his waist up—preferably around the neck—and slam him to the ground, and boy, it smarts. I'm tough. Green Bay's Boyd Dowler is going to have to watch it. I feel sorry for the guy."

—Fred Williamson, from *Life* magazine before Super Bowl I

THE NEED TO WIN

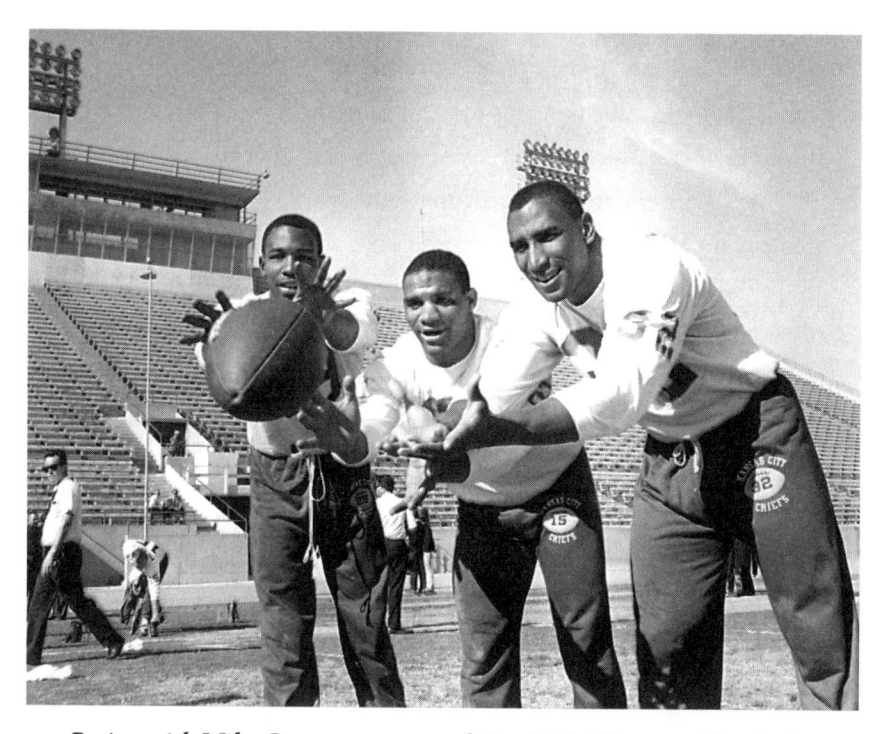

Posing with Mike Garrett, center, and Curtis McClinton, right, during practice the week before the first Super Bowl against the Packers in Los Angeles. Mike was the team's best back, and Curtis scored our only touchdown in the game. (Photo provided by AP/WWP)

Coach Stram, as well as other Chiefs officials, was incensed by the *Life* article and gave serious consideration—we found out later—to fining and suspending Freddy. Which was crap. It didn't happen, not because the team felt it wasn't the right thing to do, but because they thought it would have caused even more team dissension. Stram ultimately just warned Freddy to keep his mouth shut.

My personal preparation for the game consisted of studying the offensive game plan and concentrating on how I could beat the Packers' two great corners, Willie Wood and Herb Adderly. The play-action pass was going to be a big part of our offense—as it had been all season—and everything we planned to do would spin off that. Wood and Adderly presented a problem because they covered and defended passes so well. The more film we watched of the Packers' defense, the more obvious it was that this team of stars and super players played together very well—and that the defense was greater than the sum of its parts. Our underdog role for the game was well founded, but we remained optimistic...at least in public.

"We can beat anybody. So we're the underdog—well, underdogs have more to fight for," Stram said of our chances against Green Bay. "And we represent every player and coach in our league. That means a lot. This team will be ready."

"I don't believe the Packers are going to run us out of the park. I'd assume in an NFL area that they would make such statements. These guys don't follow us, so they don't know anything about us. How could they?"

—Len Dawson, Chiefs Quarterback, 1962-75, before Super Bowl I

Game day arrived with a bright blue sky and warm temperatures—typical Southern California weather. The war of words between the two leagues was finally going to be played out on the field. Coach Stram, in anticipation of a tense locker room before the game, had equipment manager Bobby Yarborough and trainer Wayne Rudy hunt down and wear Mickey Mouse caps—the little beanies with mouse ears on top. I guess he thought the visual reminder of the Mickey Mouse League assertions would loosen everyone up. I laughed a little, but some of the guys were put off. When you're getting ready to play the Packers, shouldn't you be a little nervous or keyed up?

As we moved through our final preparations, I made sure Yarborough got my ring and tied it to his shoelaces. Since the first exhibition game of the season, Bobby had taken care of the ring for me during games. Not knowing what to do with it initially, he tied the ring onto his shoelaces. It was a lucky ritual that we both kept going throughout the season; that ring was tied to his shoes for every game.

After Headrick completed his pregame purging, we were ready for the Packers.

The stands were only two-thirds full, which was a strange sight. The L.A. Coliseum held more than 90,000 people at the time, and the announced attendance was just over 63,000. But both CBS and NBC covered the game, and most of America tuned in.

Green Bay won the coin toss and took the ball. After getting a first down, Buck Buchanan sacked Bart Starr for a ten-yard loss. Then Bobby Bell and Jerry Mays dropped Starr again on a pass attempt. It was a good start by the defense.

We got a first down on our first possession, too, but Dawson missed me on a long third-down play and we gave the ball back to the Packers. Six plays later they had a touchdown when Starr hit old man Max McGee—who had replaced the Hammer's target Boyd Dowler because of an injury—on a 37-yard scoring pass. We moved the ball from our own 13 to the Packers' 33, but Mike Mercer missed the field-goal attempt.

And I still hadn't caught a pass.

"Every time you looked up, Otis was coasting down the sideline or running past people. We could have scored 22 touchdowns had they been watching closely at how Herb Adderley was covering Otis. He was afraid of Otis and played 10 yards off him. But we kept trying to throw slant-ins. It was crazy. If the guy is playing you ten yards off, all you have to do is catch nine-yard passes 10 times and you're 90 yards down the field. But they never threw the hitches. They kept trying to throw long, and they kept trying to throw slant-ins. They were getting Otis hit for no reason. Then, finally, Otis did catch one down the sidelines and got away from Herb Addley. I went over to

My biggest play in the first Super Bowl—I beat Willie Wood and Tom Brown on this play to set up the Chiefs' only touchdown. (Photo provided by the Kansas City Chiefs)

Coach Stram and told him, 'Look how he's playing.' Stram said, 'Don't bother me now; don't bother me now.' So I said, 'Okay, fine.'"

—Fred Williamson

Green Bay went three and out, and when we got the ball, the offense really clicked. I had my biggest play of the day on that drive, beating Willie Wood to the outside and catching a nice toss from Lenny for 31 yards. My catch put us on the Green Bay seven-yard line, and on the next play, Lenny hit Curtis McClinton in the end zone. The score was tied, 7-7. More importantly, the play-action passes were finally working.

Throughout the course of the game I found out what an outstanding cover man Willie Wood was. But was he better than the best of the AFL? In a one-game situation, it's hard to say. I think the true test of a good cornerback is how he covers you when a familiarity sets in, when you face one another several times. I beat him on my one long play, but he was solid the entire game.

Early in the second quarter, I was feeling pretty good about our chances to pull off the upset. The pregame jitters were gone, and our confidence, on both offense and defense, was high. But Starr quickly regained control of the game and marched the Packers 73 yards in 13 plays to go ahead 14-7. He had hit Carroll Dale early in the drive for a long, 64-yard score—Freddy was beaten badly on the play—but an illegal procedure penalty brought it back.

Lenny moved us down the field at the end of the quarter, and just before the half, Mercer kicked a 31-yard field goal to make the score 14-10. I caught another pass for 11 yards on that drive. We were a happy bunch of Chiefs who ran to the locker room for the break—almost too happy. We thought we had more than a chance now, and we talked about winning. The Packers, on both sides of the ball, had proved to be human after all, or so we thought, and visions of a great upset rose within us.

> *"I was in awe of [the Packers], but when I get nervous and think that people are very good and better than I am, I usually play better. And I knew I was going to play well. That didn't bother me. It's just that they were a very good team, and I was a big fan of the Packers. I looked forward to the opportunity to play against them."*
>
> —Mike Garrett, Chiefs Running Back, 1966-70

It's hard to pick out the turning point in many contests, but this game had a definite moment that the Packers took complete control. After receiving the kickoff to start the third period, we moved to midfield and faced a third down and five. The Packers blitzed, Lenny was hit as he tried to throw to Arbanas on the left side, and the ball wobbled slowly into the hands of Willie Wood, who ran it all the way back to our five-yard line. The Packers scored on the next play and went ahead 21-10.

"He should have taken the sack," Mike Garrett said later of the play. "I was yelling, 'Don't do it! Don't do it!'"

"I wish I had thrown a better pass," Lenny lamented of the interception. "I wish I had done anything except what I did. If I had thrown it outside we don't catch it, but neither do they."

And after that one bad play—our only turnover of the game—we just quit. I didn't think it was possible for that team to do, but we did. We played like the game was already lost…like a comeback was impossible. As a group, the Kansas City Chiefs dropped their heads and accepted an outcome that maybe—probably—we had predetermined for ourselves.

Green Bay scored again in the third and added a fifth touchdown in the fourth quarter. Starr and McGee were the big stars for the Packers. McGee's performance was especially great, considering he was playing on no sleep and had caught just four passes the entire season. He finished the game with seven receptions for 138 yards and two TDs, while Starr threw for 250 yards and was named the game's MVP.

The Hammer didn't break any helmets. In fact, late in the game, Green Bay's backup halfback, Donnie Anderson, accidentally kicked The Hammer in the head on a sweep and knocked him out. Freddy was carried off the field—a humiliation that would have been unbearable for almost anyone else. Freddy shook if off and didn't give it a second thought.

Finally, the game ended: Green Bay 35, Kansas City 10. The score depicts the game as a blowout. Strangely, on one hand the game was worse than the final tally reflected, while on the other hand, the score was actually closer than anyone expected.

The Packers' defense hit hard. Here I am trying to shake off the cobwebs after getting leveled during the first Super Bowl. (Photo provided by AP/WWP)

"All the talking is over now. As Hank Stram says, they beat us on the grass. They beat us physically and they used a little witchcraft on us. They're a great ball club. They're not superhuman, but they're great."

—Jerry Mays, Chiefs Defensive Lineman, 1961-70,
following the loss in Super Bowl I

I think it's safe to say the loss was more than just disappointing to everyone in the Chiefs organization. Jerry Mays took it particularly hard, and Lenny went into denial about how much better the Packers were than the Chiefs. Coach Stram, as he almost always did, expressed the frustration of our loss best, while also praising the superb talents and mastery of football that Lombardi's men displayed.

"The Packers played a great football game," Coach Stram solemnly said after the game. "They deserved to win. It's easy to understand why they have won consistently." He said a lot of other things to the media, as did many of the Chiefs. I didn't say anything and took the loss as hard anyone on the team.

And the Hammer? Freddy remained Freddy after the game.

"I guess I was knocked out," he said when questioned about the play when Anderson kneed him in the head. "I don't remember a thing. Did I make the tackle?"

The mood in the locker room after the game was strange; it didn't feel like a typical loss. There was moping and silence, but as a group I think the team was just relieved that the game was over—a feeling of surviving more than losing. I didn't think we had put forth our best effort, but the Packers stopped us from playing our best, as they did with all their opponents. Personally, I wasn't happy with my own performance of four receptions for 57 yards. I didn't do enough.

We wanted to put the game behind us, use it to improve and hopefully return to the big game the following season. But nobody let us forget about that game. It seemed like every time I turned around someone was talking about the Packers pounding us. Vince Lombardi's quotes about the NFL's superiority were in a lot of articles, and the assertions that the AFL was a joke were everywhere.

There were also implications that the Chiefs were a joke.

All through the winter and spring of 1967 we heard that crap. It got to the point where it was almost unbearable. We had lost the game, and lost big. Did we have to have our noses rubbed in it over and over?

The final, most crushing insult came when Coach Stram gathered the team together during training camp in July to watch the NFL Films highlight reel of the game. It was one of the most humiliating things I've ever had to watch. The film was more about the supposed weaknesses of the Chiefs and the AFL than it was about the Packers' superb performance. It made fun of our stack defense. It made reference to the poor play of our offensive line and Lenny, and it also made sure to take some hard hits on the Hammer. They didn't come right out and say it, but the point was clear: The Chiefs were boys pretending to be men and were pretending to play a man's game, and most specifically, we didn't belong on the same field with the Packers or any other NFL team.

If the animosity we felt for the way we were treated by the media and the NFL before and after the Super Bowl had disappeared in the six months following the game, it returned quickly. So much so that the Chiefs, collectively as a team, wanted and desperately needed retribution.

7

TUMULTUOUS TIMES

It started during the 1967 season—that's when I began to hear, on a regular basis, that I was a selfish player—and lasted right up until I retired. Some players and coaches—it always got back to me who was shooting off their mouths—started calling me self-centered. Of course, I wasn't being selfish in a bad way. I just wanted to be completely involved in the offense. If you look at everything I did in sports all the way back to high school, I simply wanted to be involved. I always had the idea that if my coaches gave me the ball I would make something good happen, and the majority of the time I did just that.

The team's success and my personal accomplishments earned me a "star" label—Otis Taylor, the big-time playmaker. And since the Chiefs were the defending AFL champs, that distinction brought high expectations for the team as a whole, but also for me from Coach Stram, Lenny, the rest of my teammates, fans, and media. Being a star also made it easier to be heard, and I realized I had the opportunity to speak my mind. But I was still finding my public voice at the time, and everything I said didn't always ring as clear as I wanted it to. I had opinions and I wanted to express them. But if you played pro football in the 1960s, you were punished for talking too much—especially if you were black. I guess I started talking too much. I really believe in my heart I was rebuked and penalized several times for showing a little resistance to what was going on socially and how the team was operating.

I would bitch about what I thought was wrong more readily than most of the players. I would open my mouth, and you know what they say, "If you'd have just kept your mouth shut, everything would have been okay." But I couldn't do that. I wasn't trying to be political; it wasn't like at all. Most of the time I was upset about what I perceived as mistreatment. Buck Buchanan always used to get on me, asking, "What's the matter with you, can't you act right?"

I would respond, "Yeah, I'm acting right. There's nothing wrong with me."

The sportswriters from the Houston area held a big dinner for me in the off season before the 1967 campaign, and, led by Lloyd Wells, many of my friends, family, coaches and teammates showed up to roast me and honor my athletic accomplishments. Coach Stram, Mr. Wells, and others gave speeches about me, and I gave a little talk, too. I thanked everyone, but I wasn't very good at telling jokes and screwed up a couple of punch lines. All in all, the dinner was a very special evening and one of the nicest things that was ever done for me.

Before I reported to training camp in the summer, I received a note from Coach Stram about the dinner. Part of that letter follows, and I've always tried to live up to his words:

> "Recognition of any kind is always appreciated, but none is more significant than the recognition received from your friends from home. I am proud to be your coach, Otis, and look forward to your helping us win many more championships. I don't expect you to be just good—I expect you to be the best!"

My family was present at the dinner and roast: Dad, Odell, Mother and me. (Photo courtesy of the Taylor Family Collection)

The Chiefs were picked by everyone to repeat as AFL champs in '67. Coach Stram began revamping the team's defense as Willie Lanier and Jim Lynch joined the club as rookies, and Jan Stenerud became our kicker. I also thought the Chiefs would repeat as champs, and I was looking forward to having an even bigger year statistically than I did in 1966. There was also the added motivation of the Super Bowl loss. A need for redemption had boiled within me and my teammates throughout the off season. Watching the Super Bowl highlight film had reignited the spark for revenge.

When the merger was originally announced, it was a good feeling, because now we were going to be one league and we'd get a chance to play against the guys who didn't think that we were good enough to be on a pro football field on Sundays. Part of the agreement when the AFL merged with the NFL was that there would be interleague exhibition games starting in '67. The Chiefs' fourth exhibition game was against the Chicago Bears in Kansas City. Nobody said anything at the time, and they didn't have to, but we were excited about the Bears coming to Kansas City. It was our chance to show the world we weren't a Mickey Mouse team.

> *"We [the Chiefs] just had a burning resentment against the NFL. We played with those same guys in college, and they weren't that different. Our talent level was high, and it got better in 1967 when we picked up Jan Stenerud and Willie Lanier. Our team was stronger, and when we went into that game with the Bears, we were so ready to play you wouldn't believe it."*
>
> —Chris Burford

One thing about our exhibition games and Hank Stram: We always played to win. Always. Coach Stram felt that if we were going to play, then we should play to win. He also believed that winning was contagious and would springboard the team into the regular season with a positive attitude. Our first exhibition game was against the Oilers in Houston, and we won, 24-9. After that, we traveled to Birmingham, Alabama (that was something the AFL did a lot in the 1960s—play exhibition games all over the country) and beat the Jets, and to Portland, Oregon, where we whipped the Raiders, 48-0. And then, the NFL, represented by the Chicago Bears, came to Kansas City.

We were ready for them.

I know I carried a grudge about the Green Bay loss from the time we read the newspapers and magazines after the Super Bowl until summer camp started the following year. It's hard to believe, but before the game with the Bears we didn't talk about kicking their asses in the locker room. We just felt that if we played our game of football, we would beat the hell out of them. It was funny to me because I knew we were going to stomp them. I couldn't wait until they sang the national anthem and we took the field.

The Bears moved right down the field on their first possession and eventually kicked a field goal. We actually floundered a bit on offense initially, but then Lenny and I hooked up for a 70-yard touchdown play at the end of the first quarter. Dawson threw to Curtis McClinton for the two-point conversion—a rule the NFL didn't have. Chris Burford took an 11-yard pass in for a score, Mike Garrett scored and I caught a 29-yard touchdown pass. The score was 39-10 at the half, and we poured it on in the second half as well—it was a rout. The Chiefs had a horse called Warpaint who ran around the field, circled and came back when we scored. We damn near ran that poor horse to death that night.

When the game ended it was Chiefs 66, Bears 24.

"[The Chiefs] gave every indication tonight that they could play as good as any team in the National Football League," Papa Bear

George Halas said following the massacre of his team. "They were fired up, played with great spirit and gave 100 percent on every play."

Gale Sayers, the Bears' great running back, who didn't have much of a game, wasn't as impressed. "I would compare the Chiefs to the Rams," he said. "They were big across the front like L.A. Things went their way."

"They had Gale Sayers, Dick Butkus, Johnny Morris, Doug Atkins— they were in the NFL championship game three years before. I'm coming back from a route downfield and Richie Petitbon, who was a good safety for them, says, 'Hey Chris, when are you guys going to lay off?' I remember telling him, 'Not tonight, Richie. Not tonight.' We just poured it on. That was when both teams were on the same side of the field [at Municipal Stadium]. After the game, George Halas walked off the field and he had tears in his eyes. That was the worst beating the Bears ever had in the history of their club—66 to 24. It was one of those things—you wrung it all out of your system. We'd taken so much abuse. The Denver Broncos were still the poorest team in our league at that time, and they beat the Detroit Lions. That was the first interleague exhibition game, Detroit and Denver. And then we played the Bears and just killed them. That kind of changed people's perception of the AFL a little bit."

—Chris Burford

I have to say that, to a man, every player on the team who participated in that Bears game thinks it was the greatest game ever played by the Chiefs. It doesn't matter that it was an exhibition game. It matters that it was the NFL, and we got our much-needed revenge. I left the anger and bitterness behind me when the Chicago game ended.

Why weren't we able to focus and play like that in the Super Bowl? Were the Packers more intimidating than the Bears? I think it was just a big mind thing. What everyone always forgets about that Bears game is that we traveled to Los Angeles the following week and played the Rams in the Coliseum—the site of the Super Bowl game with the Packers. We were understandably flat and lost, 44-24. The strange thing about the game with the Rams is that there were more people at the exhibition game—73,990—than there were at the Super Bowl.

The 1967 season turned out to be a big disappointment. I don't think we left "it" on the field with Chicago, but we did leave behind seven months of harassment, seven months of listening to people tell us we got our asses whipped, and seven months of hearing we weren't able to play the same brand of football the NFL guys were playing. Maybe that was the problem.

By doing what we did to Chicago, we proved to the world we weren't as bad as they said we were and could play with anybody. And we let our guard down.

We didn't play well that season, at least not up to our potential week after week. And I don't think I necessarily played well. We won our first two games, 25-20, at Houston, and then we blanked the Dolphins in Miami, 24-0. The third game of the season was against the Raiders in Oakland. It was a big game, but I doubt anyone on the team knew how much of an effect it would have on our entire season.

It was the type of game that became standard in the Chiefs-Raiders rivalry—fierce hitting, tough defense, and big plays. The Raiders jumped to a 10-0 lead and we had to play catchup the rest of the game. After falling behind 16-7 in the third, Lenny hit me for a 17-yard touchdown, and, following another Raiders score, we pulled within two when Mike Garrett ran it in. Both of those TDs were set up by Noland Smith kickoff returns of 54 and 48 yards. When our defense got the ball back on our own 20-yard line with two minutes remaining in the game, we had one last shot to pull out the win. Lenny sent me long down the left side of the field. I beat my man badly, but Lenny's pass was a tad underthrown. I slowed just past midfield; the ball hit me right in the hands, and...I dropped it.

We lost the game, 23-21. I don't think I could have scored a touchdown on the play, but we would have been in easy field goal range. Dropping that pass was one of the worst plays of my career. I let my teammates, my coaches and myself down. The Chiefs never recovered from that loss, and, just like in that game, we had to play catchup the rest of the season. The Raiders were just sensational in 1967. They finished 13-1 (beating us 44-22 in KC) and whipped Houston in the AFL championship game. Then they got the same treatment from the Packers in the Super Bowl that we received the year before, losing 33-14. The Chiefs finished 9-5, but we could easily have been 12-2. I had good numbers, 59 receptions for 958 yards and 11 TDs, but I know I didn't play as well as I had in 1966. It was a most disappointing season.

"The pleasurable—but also unpleasant—burden of being a citizen and getting your ass kicked at the same time while performing at championship level is a Herculean task. We never had the enjoyment of counting money, because it just wasn't in the game. And if we had the money at the time we came here, we wouldn't have had any place to stay past 27th Street because we were black boys. That never affected our ability to perform. But what it built into the character of Otis Taylor and the other guys is that we would kick your ass on the field, and the evolution of that was that we knew there was parity and the ability to perform at the highest level of our character, not only on the field, but in society. Therefore, we basically dealt with the skill, the development of life and parity, equality and championship, living in this world before we die in that microcosm of those years, and Otis Taylor was a part of that. We were tempered in steel and no

The Champ—I first met Muhammad Ali, left, in 1966 with teammate Gene Thomas, center. Ali is, without a doubt, the greatest. (Photo courtesy of the Taylor Family Collection)

> *matter what great strength we had, we're not assimilated with equality, love and passion from a country we fought and died for and educated ourselves for. Otis Taylor comes out of that era. It was our stake in our society of the game we played, the city we played in and what we prepared ourselves in college to do."*
>
> —Curtis McClinton

I first met Muhammad Ali when he fought Cleveland Williams in Houston in 1966. Once again it was Lloyd Wells who was responsible for that, and it was quite a thrill for me. Ali called me "Big O," and at one point in that initial conversation he said, referring to guarding me on the football field, "I could catch you; you wouldn't score a point against me." Then he pointed to the ring (we were in his training facility) and told me he could take me any time in there, too.

I actually did a little boxing myself at the YMCA in Houston, right down by Texas Southern, and I hung out there a lot. They had a boxing club, and I got whipped to death by the boys in the gym. Damn, they hit hard—I knew boxing was not for me.

When I touched Ali's hand it was like receiving an electrical shock. The man is so pure, he radiates from head to toe. And when you touch him, it's like nothing you have experienced before. That man thought he was great; without a doubt, he thought he was the greatest thing on this earth. I have to agree with him.

Look at how much he had to go through because he didn't serve in the military; think about how much he lost. He was called everything from un-American to traitor, and most ridiculous of all, ungrateful for what his country had done for him. We're not talking about a 30- or 35-year-old man who has the experience and wisdom only age can give an individual, we're talking about a young man who was my age at the time, 25. All he had to do was say okay, receive an easy duty and resume his boxing career. His refusal to fight—or condone the fighting and Vietnam War—really says something about his inner strength. He lost everything, but really lost nothing.

While he refused the draft and refused induction, I just got pissed—absolutely and completely mad at what was going on. I also got a note from the government at that time, and my classification number could have gotten me drafted because they had stopped giving exemptions. But that's part of the service. I had the choice of waiting to see if I'd get called up or joining the reserves. I joined the air force, but Ali stuck to his convictions. He chose to stand on what his religious beliefs were and asked for an exemption. I don't think

Meeting presidential candidate Hubert H. Humphrey in 1968 with Chiefs great Buck Buchannan, right. (Photo courtesy of the Taylor Family Collection)

there's a man on this earth who could have done what he did, come back after it was all over, and eventually carry the torch for the United States in the Olympic games. You can't beat that. You can say a lot of things about Muhammad Ali, but he's a good person and a great man.

"All of the African-American Chiefs players—Otis Taylor, Mike Garrett, Bobby Bell, Willie Lanier, myself and all the others, we were in a different time. The assimilation of Kansas City, and the city's love for the Chiefs and the integration of the city itself from the private sector responding to the needs of the players regarding work and jobs, you're talking about talented guys in that whole area who were preparing themselves for the real world. There was a weaving of geographical areas. You get a guy like Mike Garrett who comes in from California, and he really had no tolerance or patience at all in regard to what had changed immensely when he got here. There were times when he made me feel like an Uncle Tom because maybe I was too tolerant in trying to be collaborative and work through society as it was in its segregated state, or its limited state, in regard to the off-the-field acceptance of black athletes. And that was good, because Mike came from the West Coast. He opened up our heads and thinking."

—Curtis McClinton

When Martin Luther King was assassinated on April 4, 1968, racial rioting broke out across the United States. It was already a volatile time in the country—the Vietnam War continued to escalate with no end in sight—and the great civil rights leader had been responsible for many of the positive changes made concerning African Americans and other minorities in the past decade. But change almost never comes easy, and with the death of Dr. King, it certainly wasn't coming cheap.

The assassination was on a Thursday, and by the end of the weekend, almost every major city was in violent turmoil. Many cities were counting the rising death tolls and assessing property damage, but Kansas City had yet to experience any real trouble. Monday passed and still KC remained calm.

On the Tuesday following the assassination, Curtis McClinton, Buck Buchanan, Fred Williamson and myself were scheduled (well in advance of the assassination) to present information about the Negro Industrial and Economic Union to the students at Central, Paseo, Lincoln and Southwest high schools in the Kansas City district. We started at Central High, and after Curtis sang the Lord's Prayer and read a tribute to Dr. King, we found out that the other schools had been dismissed, and a march downtown was set to begin. McClinton and I went to the Troost Lake area to talk to the leaders of the march. We asked them to be peaceful and reminded them that Dr. King would have been peaceful.

Kansas City Mayor Ilus Davis joined us then, and we marched with the students. Personally, the only thing I did was talk to them and I asked them to settle down. I wanted them to know that we—the Chiefs players—would help if they were peaceful. I don't know how effective I was, but I know I wasn't scared to get out there and do it because I knew it had to be done. Buck and Freddy joined us in the march, and when we got to city hall, the four of us joined with civic leaders and again appealed for nonviolent behavior. It appeared to work, but when the crowd began to disperse, a tear gas bomb exploded, and everything went to hell. Kansas City was ravaged with rioting and violence for the next few days.

When the riots finally ended, the city had sustained six deaths, many injuries and hundreds of thousands of dollars of property damage. Across the country, the death toll from the riots was staggering: Chicago 11, Washington seven, Baltimore six, Detroit two. It was the ugliest of times for the country and for Kansas City. The scars from the violence took a while to heal, but things got better, and the city became a better place for all its citizens.

The Kansas City Chiefs played a big part in race relations throughout the late 1960s in the metropolitan area. We brought people together when they came to our games—they may not have wanted to touch each other initially, but sitting together in the stands was a tremendous start. The sad reality was that people could interact and talk about the game on Sunday, but couldn't sit together on the bus. I think we had a hell of a group of black men on this team who played a big part in bringing people together. We didn't have a pulpit to talk from, so we just talked to people on street. Nobody asked us to do anything—we just did it.

"It was a very difficult time when the Chiefs first came to Kansas City. Black people could not live past 27th Street. Abner Haynes and I went out together to an affair that we were invited to on the Plaza, and they told us we couldn't come in. They would not serve us anything, not even water, so we left. The situation of the players was improving in that era, probably more so in '63, '64 and '65 because things were beginning to change concerning accommodations and other things. I lived in the basement of a house that was next to the church I belong to now. And that neighborhood was my neighborhood because I was really awed and surprised by the segregation in Kansas City. I think what I am really trying to say is that there was duress on the players during those years. It wasn't an issue of a comfort index as far as the ability to live, but there was an extreme amount of pressure in dual comprehension of the player on the field, the team, the love for that organization and the overall duality of society transitioning to the point where we had the assassination of Martin Luther King. All of us—the players on the Chiefs—were champions in a non-championship time, in a non-championship environment in the United States of America, especially in Kansas City.

Blowing past a Boston Patriots defender and making the play. (Photo provided by AP/WWP)

"On the Tuesday prior to the riots in Kansas City, we were at Central High. We had been involved with the Black Economic Industrial Union with Jim Brown and founded a chapter in Kansas City. We were at the high school in reference and respect to the assassination of King. As we were speaking—I don't remember who the speaker was, if I was speaking or just on the stage—we watched the students walk out of the auditorium and proceed to downtown. Now the uniqueness of all that is that when we saw the students leave the auditorium, we didn't know where in the world they were going. When we got out, we began to follow them, and did so all the way from Central High School to 18th and Paseo, 18th and Vine. Kansas City's Mayor Davis met us there. We tried to keep those kids from heading downtown, but we all began to get scattered; I got scattered. I'm sure the other guys from the Chiefs were dispersed, but I ended up downtown. I actually got shot with a pellet bullet. Anyway, something hit me in the chest and I didn't know what it was at the time. When I got hit, I left because I realized the situation had gone beyond my broadest comprehension."

—Curtis McClinton

Here I am doing my best to look tough and intimidating. (Photo provided by AP/WWP)

The main thing I remember about the 1968 season is pain. It seemed like I was never 100 percent for any of the games, even though I know I was. I pulled my groin muscle, and I had never experienced such excruciating pain before. The worst thing about a groin injury is that there is nothing you can do for it, really, except wait for it to heal. And the waiting was almost a bad as the pain.

It was the fourth game of the season—a Saturday night affair in Miami. We beat the Dolphins easily, 48-3. But in the third quarter, while making a routine block, I pulled my groin muscle. At that point in the season I had just 15 receptions, but was still the top receiver on the team. Coach Stram was running the ball more than ever, and with his revamped defense, the Chiefs were once again one of the top teams in the league. We lost the second game of the season to the Jets at home by one point—one stinking point. Namath ran out the final six-plus minutes of the game to seal the win for New York. That one game kept us from winning the division outright.

I would catch only five more passes the rest of the season, but the team didn't need me nearly as much that year. Stram used a T-formation running attack against the Raiders and ran them into the ground at Municipal Stadium, 24-10. At the end of the season we had a 12-2 record—the best regular-season winning percentage in the club's history. The problem was that the Raiders were also 12-2. A divisional playoff was set up—in Oakland, of course—to determine who would play the Jets for the AFL championship.

We could have saved everyone a lot of trouble and money by just giving the title to the Raiders. They jumped on us immediately, scoring 21 points in the first quarter, and routed us thoroughly, 41-6. We really stank up the Oakland Coliseum. It was an embarrassing ending to a superb season, but looking back, I think the team wasn't quite ready to make the big step back to the championship level.

The Jets defeated the Raiders for the AFL championship and then shocked the sports world by upsetting the Baltimore Colts in Super Bowl III. I was elated, and I guarantee you that every player in the AFL went home in the off season talking and bragging about the New York Jets and Joe Willie Namath. Namath, as one man, set the tone for a greater football product. The players on the Kansas City Chiefs couldn't have been any prouder of the Jets' accomplishment if we had won the game against the Colts ourselves. And when we began preparing for the 1969 season the following summer, we kept that feeling in mind.

8

"THAT'S MY BABY!"

The tiny locker room at Tulane Stadium in New Orleans was overcrowded and jubilant, bordering on delirious euphoria. Whooping, yelling, and undecipherable shouts echoed around and off the walls. People were packed together tightly, but it bothered no one. Television and newspaper reporters were intertwined thickly throughout the happy group of football players, interviewing anyone and everyone.

It was just 10 minutes after the Kansas City Chiefs' 23-7 victory over the Minnesota Viking in Super Bowl IV, and while my teammates, coaches and everyone connected to the Chiefs' organization were expressing their joy in the most extroverted of ways, I was trying to collect myself for an interview. The Kansas City Chiefs were the world champions of professional football, and my happiness had gotten the best of my emotions.

I was crying.

• • •

Taking the field at Municipal Stadium before a game in 1969. I'm zoned in, wearing my game face and ready to play. (Photo provided by the Kansas Collection, U. of Kansas Archives)

Long before the 1969 season began, I thought we had the stuff to return to the Super Bowl, despite the disastrous season-ending loss to the Raiders in '68, and I was very upbeat when I reported to training camp. We had all the parts in place—everybody was healthy, fired up and ready to play. The team immediately had that championship feeling, maybe because we were so close to it the year before. With my groin injury a thing of the past, I was ready to burst out and again make major contributions to the team.

My receiver's mentality was rejuvenated.

I guess you could call 1969 one of our most intense seasons from start to finish. Coach Stram, acting even more authoritative than usual, laid down the law early in training camp—no long hair, no sideburns, no facial hair. A $500 fine was waiting for anyone who broke the rules. It was rigid, but effective. Our close team got even tighter.

Jim Marsalis, a rookie from Tennessee State, took over at left cornerback and immediately made our defense—already one of the best in pro football—even better with his tremendous coverage skills in the secondary. On offense, we were still going to have wide open plays, multiple sets and play-action passes, but the running game would be the center of our attack. As always I wanted the ball as much as I could get it, but I also wanted to win. I knew my blocking skills would be just as important as catching the ball.

We breezed through our exhibition games, finishing with a perfect 6-0 record in the preseason. The regular season started in San Diego, and we won, 27-9. The next week in Boston we blanked the Patriots and won easily, 31-0, but paid an enormous price in the game. Lenny took a hit on his knee in the third quarter and was out for a least a month. When the team traveled to Cincinnati the following week, we also lost our backup quarterback, Jacky Lee, when he broke an anklebone. That meant Mike Livingston, a second-year quarterback who saw just five minutes of playing time in 1968, was our new starting quarterback. The Bengals, who were only in their second year of existence, beat us that day, 24-19. The balance of the season seemed to be in doubt.

As it turned out, the entire team moved forward without a hitch. Livingston, who played his college ball at SMU, was a bit of a runner and had a strong throwing arm—a good player all around. He took over as the starter the following week at Denver and played some beautiful football as we beat the Broncos, 26-13. Everybody, including me, worked harder than we ever had in practice the rest of the season. Mike needed to have the confidence that we were behind him. Since we didn't know when Lenny was coming back, everybody on the team made sure Livingston knew that he was our man. Mike was just terrific, and we won the next three games in a row. Lenny, who decided against surgery on his knee, was able to play in our next game against the Bills, which we won, 29-7.

> *"He made so many fantastic catches it's hard to single out one. He made a lot of one-hand catches—a lot of catches with three, four guys on him. He's the strongest wide receiver I've ever seen-one guy couldn't tackle him, they couldn't get him down. I remember the Miami game in 1969 when we hooked up for a 93-yard touchdown, he told me he could beat this guy to the post and the free safety was getting beaten up and had no respect in center field. So I threw him a good pass and he made a great run. They had a real fast guy in their defensive secondary, but he couldn't get him down—couldn't tackle him—and Otis lateraled back to Robert Holmes, who took it the final 15 yards or so into the end zone."*

—Mike Livingston, Chiefs Quarterback, 1968-79

The Chiefs then stood at 7-1 for the season, and Dawson started against the Chargers at Municipal in the next game. We won easily, 27-3, and Lenny played as well as he ever had. Next on the schedule were the Jets, the defending world champs, in New York. Ready to resume his starting role at quarterback, fate struck a harsh blow to Lenny when his father died the Friday before the game. He decided to play—I can't express how much respect his teammates had for him because of that. Filled with sorrow from his dad's death, Lenny was brilliant against the Jets, throwing for 285 yards, including three touchdown passes to me. We flattened the Jets, 34-16, and made the cover of *Sports Illustrated*.

And then the Oakland Raiders came to Kansas City.

*Lenny the Cool, preparing to pass in Super Bowl IV.
(Photo provided by the Kansas City Chiefs)*

At that point in the season, the Chiefs were 9-1, the Raiders 8-1-1. If we won the game, we would almost assuredly win the division, but the postseason was different that year. The AFL had a new playoff system for its final season of existence and expanded from two to four teams. The two division winners would play the second-place team from the other division in a "Divisional Playoff." The two winning teams would then play for the AFL title. So the Oakland contest was the biggest game of the year. Winning our division would mean home field advantage in the playoffs, and with Lenny back at quarterback, we thought we were ready for the Raiders—we weren't. In front of a sold-out Municipal Stadium crowd, we played our worst game of the year—seven turnovers, including two interceptions returned for touchdowns. We handed the Raiders the game, 27-24, as well as first place.

"Like they say, when everything goes well, it goes well," Jim Marsalis said after the loss to the Raiders in Kansas City. "When it doesn't, the handle comes off the pump and the water begins to flow."

We came back against the Broncos on Thanksgiving, winning 31-17, but Lenny tweaked his knee again in that game. Livingston took the snaps in the next game against Buffalo, and we eked out a 22-19 win as Jan Stenerud nailed five field goals—the final kick was the game winner with two minutes left. That left us with a big showdown in the final contest of the season at Oakland; the winning team would take the division title, the loser would have to play the Jets in New York in the first round of the playoffs.

Because of Lenny's weak knee, the game plan devised by Coach Stram was extremely conservative. We were going to run the ball to minimize the strength of the Raiders' secondary and play for field position. The plan was good to a point; we controlled the ball but couldn't score. The Raiders kicked a first-half field goal; Stenerud missed his attempt. After Oakland got a touchdown early in the fourth quarter, we ran a long, time-consuming 15-play drive and finally scored. Garrett was stopped trying to go in for a two-point conversion, and the Raiders ran the clock out after that. Final score: Oakland 10, Kansas City 6. The loss left the Chiefs in second place in the Western Division with an 11-3 record; the Raiders finished in first at 12-1-1.

The biggest problem with that game was that we only threw six passes. Six passes! Lenny said afterward that he had no idea he threw so few; he was simply following the game plan. Stram was widely criticized for the loss, and he took every bit of it, never second-guessing himself. A lot of my teammates were upset, and rightly so, about the ultra-conservative play calling.

"I knew if we didn't succeed I would be criticized," Stram said to the press after the tough loss. "If you want to win a popularity contest you can throw the ball, do everything, and if you lose Dawson you have insulated yourself with an excuse to fail."

I was a non-factor in our offense the entire game, as were Pitts, Arbanas and Richardson, the other receivers. The hardest part to swallow about the loss is that we now had to play the Jets in New York in the first round of the playoffs. The Raiders were paired against the much easier Houston Oilers at home.

Despite our run-oriented attack, I was pleased with my personal performance and overall contributions to the team's success during the 1969 regular season. I caught 41 passes for 696 yards and seven touchdowns and had several big plays. Garrett led the team in receptions with 43 and rushing yards with 732. As a team, the Chiefs threw just 351 passes and ran the ball 522 times, but we won, and with an inexperienced quarterback.

When we went to New York for the divisional playoff, we were thinking we had three more games to play. Forget about the cliché "Play one game at a time." The Chiefs were looking at the New York game as the first of a three-part goal. And we expected to win.

Shea Stadium was cold and windswept on game day, and even though we had easily ripped the Jets just a month earlier, we knew we were in for tough game. Our offense had clicked in our previous meeting, but this game turned into a defensive struggle. By the fourth quarter we had a slim 6-3 lead, but Joe Namath had his team at the goal line with a first down following a pass interference call in the end zone, ready to take the lead.

I've never been much for defense and defensive players, but what followed was one of the greatest sequences I've ever seen in a clutch game situation. Jets running back Bill Mathis was stopped for no gain on first down, and Matt Snell lost half a yard on the next play. On third down, Namath faked a pitch, faked a handoff, and turned to his right to throw to Snell. But Bobby Bell ended up right in Namath's face, and he forced a poor pass that fell harmlessly to the ground. New York had to settle for a field goal, which tied the score.

We didn't wait long to take back the lead. Lenny and I hooked up on a 61-yard pass play that put the ball on New York's 19, and on the next play, Gloster hauled in the go-ahead touchdown. Our defense shut down Namath the rest of the way, and we had earned our way back to the AFL Championship game—Kansas City 13, New York 6.

"If you get close to Joe Namath and say 'Jim Marsalis,' I'll bet he flinches. I had two interceptions in that [1969 Divisional Playoff], and I got one when they were going in for a score. They were going to throw a quick slant on the goal line, and I picked the ball off. I picked one off earlier in the game and that led to Gloster's touchdown."

—Jim Marsalis, Chiefs Defensive Back, 1969-75

•••

"I didn't know that was going to be the next play—my touchdown reception against the Jets. Dawson called the play from the huddle. I

guess he saw something in the back and he called for it to come to me. I guess he wanted to set it up with Otis, but he had just gone to Otis on the previous play. I'm sure Otis would have caught the pass if he had been in there, but it really helped that I saw what he did to get open on the pass prior to mine. So, like I said, I always watched this guy. I stayed focused on him all the time because he was just fun to watch."

—Gloster Richardson

The Raiders humiliated the Oilers the next day, 56-7, and we had another date in Oakland. The problem was that the Raiders had beaten us seven out the last eight times we played. And that was embarrassing—we were tired of getting whipped by those guys. I felt that the last time we played them we could have won, but we were playing not to lose instead of trying to win. I don't think Coach Stram realized his conservative game had us playing scared.

On the plane ride to Oakland the guys were serious, all business. We were so tired of losing to the Raiders. We had two weeks to prepare for the game—a long time—but we were still ready, mentally and physically. I'm pretty sure they underestimated us, and we had counted on that. Stram pieced together another semi-conservative game plan, but Lenny was going to be able to throw a lot more than he had in the previous game.

Once again, the Raiders scored first; once again, we had to play from behind. But this game was different, and we all knew it. George Blanda, the Raiders' aging kicker, missed two field goal attempts, and when Wendell Hayes scored on a one-yard touchdown run in the second quarter, we were tied at the half, 7-7.

Blanda missed another field goal early in the second half, and shortly after that Lenny and I hooked up on one of the biggest plays of the season. With the ball on the Raiders' two-yard line and facing a third and 14, Lenny was flushed to his right on a pass play. I ran down the right side of the field, but Lenny was looking for Robert Holmes. When he started to run out of time, he threw for me. I had to catch the ball as it came in—reaching out and one-handing it. I pulled it in and covered up. It was one of my better catches, especially considering the pressure of the situation and game. We moved the ball to the Raiders' 32-yard line after that, and when Lenny threw to me at the Raiders seven, we caught a break when pass interference was called on my defender. Three plays later, Holmes scored the go-ahead touchdown, and we never looked back.

There was a strange sequence of plays in the fourth quarter—we intercepted a pass from Oakland quarterback Daryle Lamonica, then fumbled the ball right back to Oakland; then we intercepted again and again fumbled it right back. Finally, Emmitt Thomas picked off another Raider pass and returned it 62 yards to set up a Stenerud field goal that put the game out of reach. The final AFL championship belonged to the Chiefs-Kansas City 17, Oakland 7.

We had finally beaten those guys and beaten them when it hurt the most. We were going back to the Super Bowl and getting another shot at the NFL in a game that really mattered.

"That year Oakland came to Kansas City and beat us. We went to Oakland and they beat us again. Well, they figured they had our number. They were really the only team that could do anything with us, and they ended up beating us twice, so they won the division and got the home-field advantage in the playoffs. We end up going to New York to play the Jets. And the Jets said they were going to pound us, but we took care of them. The Raiders figured, 'They're coming back out? Oh my God, this is easy.' I remember this: We went out there and decided there was no way—no way—that team could beat us three times in one year. No way. And Coach Stram said, "We're going to go out there and play basic football against those guys. We're

going to take it to them." And that's what we did—on defense, on offense. We ran two tight ends at one time. We just played them heads-up. They were stumped. They figured they were just going to walk right through us. The next thing you know, they turned the ball over a couple times; we capitalized, and came up with seven points.

"I think Emmitt [Thomas] intercepted a couple passes on them—stopped them right there at the goal line. I think Al Davis told his coaches and players that the game was going to be so easy that when they came to the game to bring their bags for the trip to the Super Bowl. So all the Raiders packed their bags and came to the game. We went in there and beat them. We found out about the Raiders' packed bags while we sat in the bus outside the gate after the game and had to wait for the Raiders players to come and get them. That was so funny, those guys coming out with their suitcases packed to go to the Super Bowl, and they had to go back home."

—Bobby Bell

•••

"Otis made the big plays, you know. The man had great speed. We used him in a lot of positions. We used him in a position between a guard and a tackle a lot during the course of the season. Nobody knew where he was and we would run a quick pass play, popping him through there for a big gain. The Jets didn't know until Tuesday, I don't think, where he came from. I don't mean to be critical of the Jets, but that's what happened. And he made a great one-handed catch against the Raiders in the game that we won to earn the right to go to the Super Bowl. How he caught that ball, I don't know."

—Hank Stram

On the Tuesday before Super Bowl IV as we were making our preparations to play the Minnesota Vikings, NBC news reported that Lenny was going to be called to testify before a justice department task force grand jury in Detroit as part of a gambling investigation. His name was included in a list of phone numbers held by a Donald Dawson—no relation to Lenny—who was a pretty notorious gambler. I guess he was nothing more than a casual acquaintance of Lenny's, a guy he'd met some 10 years before in Pittsburgh. Donald Dawson had called Len when he hurt his knee and also when his father died. Six other pro football players and college coach were named in the investigation, including Joe Namath.

Between 1966 and 1968, almost every Chiefs game was off the betting line in Las Vegas. There was a big inquiry, but nothing came of it, except they asked Lenny to take a lie-detector test in 1968; he did, and he passed easily. But these new allegations, reported during Super Bowl week, caught everyone off guard, and I know it bothered Lenny a lot. And it also upset his family a great deal. At the beginning, we weren't even sure if he was going to play on Sunday.

One of the things about the bogus reporting that I remember best is Joe Namath coming out in support of Lenny. Namath wasn't playing the Super Bowl, of course, and he didn't have a family at the time, so being named wasn't a big deal to him. But he knew it was to Lenny, and his public statement to that effect was a classy thing for him to do.

Here's a little bit about Lenny—about how I feel about him and how his teammates felt about him. Lenny was the Chiefs' number-one quarterback—really the heart and soul of the team—for my entire playing career. He was called "Lenny the Cool," simply because he was. Nothing ever rattled him. He'd had the misfortune of not getting a fair shot in the NFL with Cleveland and Pittsburgh and was washed out after five seasons on the bench. When Coach Stram brought him to Dallas, all Lenny did was lead the Texans to the AFL title in the first of his true Hall of Fame seasons. He and I always got along very well. We always talked football and he wanted my input on what patterns I thought would work best in the course of any particular game.

Lenny was always our leader, and the Chiefs players respected him. He didn't have a great athletic body, and if you looked at him in the prime of his great career, you'd never think he was a football player. We used to tease him about it, how he looked more like a clubhouse boy than a pro quarterback. But he was our leader, and we followed. And it wasn't just because he was the quarterback. His presence on the field made us better. His voice had a calming effect on the team. He had to be our leader. It wasn't something he took on his own or asked for—we gave it to him. We, meaning the rest of the guys on the Chiefs, selected him. He was the man.

Was he a great quarterback? Hell, yes. Could he throw it as hard as a Brett Favre or John Elway? As far as Peyton Manning? No. But he threw it perfectly and accurately. He always got me the ball. He did his job and I did my job, and we were a successful tandem. I think we made each other better players, and you can't ask for more on the football field. Lenny has also made it known around circles in and out of the NFL that I should be in the Hall of Fame, and he doesn't have to say or do anything like that.

So how big a distraction to our game preparation for the Super Bowl was the gambling story? None. And that's when I knew for sure that we had a good team. We hung loose, even though we practiced with security—with police surrounding the field. We were asked to notify them if anybody approached us or had meetings about what was expected of us. We were given a daily report of what was happening with Lenny, and the first two or three days weren't that good because the national news was really talking about it—that he had bet some money on games and he had done something in college.

I just caught a seven-yard hitch pass from Lenny, and I'm about to leave Minnesota's Earsell Mackbee on the ground...

I race down the sideline.

... and leave the Vikings' Paul Krause behind as I run for the final, decisive touchdown for Super Bowl IV. I put a good move on Krause that allowed me to dance into the end zone. (Photos on this page provided by The Topeka C-J)

They went all the way back to when he was at Purdue, trying to find some connection to the gambling investigation.

The other thing about that week was that nobody—especially the football experts—thought we could win the game. No one gave us a chance. We were 13-point underdogs—just what everyone needed, more gambling stuff—and that was ridiculous. The Vikings were a good team, but I knew we were much better. I was very nervous about the game, but fired up.

It was overcast and wet in New Orleans when the game started. When we left the dressing room, we were determined not to be embarrassed by an NFL team again. We just took it right to them. While our defense shut Joe Kapp and his Vikings offense down, we were able to move the ball. Stenerud booted a 48-yard field goal to give us a 3-0 led, and he kicked two more to put us up 9-0 in the second quarter. When the Vikings fumbled the kickoff following the third field goal, we recovered on Minnesota's 19-yard line. Three plays later, Lenny hit me at the four-yard line, and we had a first and goal. When Garrett ran the ball into the end zone a couple of plays later—65 toss power trap—the Chiefs were ahead 16-0. That was the score at the half.

The Vikings started the second half by stopping us and then driving 69 yards for a touchdown. It looked like they might be back in the game. Following their score, we got the ball at our own 18, and five plays later we were at the Minnesota 46. Throughout the game Lenny had thrown several successful short out-patterns—six or seven yards—to Pitts and me. The Vikings' secondary was hanging back, giving us the play for most of the game. Lenny called it again, to me on the right side. I made my break, turned and caught the pass. Earlier in the game after catching a short out-pass I had turned back to the inside of the field, but this time—purely by instinct—I turned quickly to the outside when the Vikings' Earsell Mackbee hit me. I left him lying on the ground.

THE NEED TO WIN

I bolted down the sideline, and Paul Krause, Minnesota's safety, tried to cut me off and run me out of bounds around the 20-yard line. I made a move toward him—it was almost like a shock wave—faking that I was going to come back across the field, but I kept my balance and went straight ahead, staying in bounds. He didn't touch me. I kept running and pranced like a horse into the end zone. I wasn't showing off; I was just happy to score. That 46-yard touchdown catch and run was the biggest single play of my career.

There was 1:22 left in the third quarter, and we knew then that we would win the game.

The most beautiful thing about that game and that play was that my Mom was there to see it. When I scored that touchdown, I heard her voice in the crowd yelling, "That's my baby, that's my baby!" I could actually hear her voice. It brought tears to my eyes then, and it brings tears to them whenever I think about her now, because she was so special to me. She wanted everybody to know whose baby it was who scored. I was really happy to get back to the sideline and hear that voice. I couldn't see her, but I could hear her.

> *"Otis was such a strong guy—he could do anything. So when the Minnesota guy missed him and he ran down the field [for the touchdown], that was a great play. And all I could think was: Otis can do anything. He can run, he can catch, he can block-he could do it all. Nothing Otis did surprised me. I was definitely happy when he made that touchdown because it put us in the driver's seat and, I think, was the decider of the game."*
>
> —Mike Garrett

After my touchdown, our defense really started to pound Kapp and the rest of the Minnesota offense. Buck, Willie Lanier, Jerry Mays, Bobby Bell, Aaron Brown and Curly Culp—those guys just beat the crap out of the Vikings. We pretty much ran the ball the rest of the game and waited for the clock to run out—why not? On our last series of the game, right before he was replaced by Mike Livingston, Lenny rolled out to his right on a little pass play and was tackled by Carl Eller. While he was still on the ground, Alan Page, one of the Vikings' big linemen, speared Lenny in the back—a dirty shot if there ever was one. Both benches emptied, but Lenny coolly walked away, always in control. Mike Livingston replaced him on the next play and handed the ball off twice, and then the Chiefs were the world champs—Kansas City 23, Minnesota 7.

The Jets and Raiders were better teams than Minnesota. I know so for sure, and I think there were a lot of teams in the AFL who were better than the Vikings. They were a running team—very one-dimensional—and while their defense wasn't bad, it wasn't anything special. Of the three playoff games we played that year, the Vikings game was by far the easiest one for the Chiefs.

> *"We just dominated Minnesota offensively and defensively. We really had a strong defense, and I think our defense really won the championship. But you have to put points on the board. Thank God for Len Dawson and Otis Taylor. That was kind of a funny thing. I remember when Otis was drawing in the dirt—a play. That was kind of funny, to me anyway, because they were both serious, but here Otis was drawing a play in the dirt that wasn't really in the game plan—he was making up his own play."*
>
> —Ed Budde

In the crowded locker room following the game, shouts and hugs were everywhere.

"This is a much greater thrill than anything that has ever happened," Lamar Hunt, the Chiefs' owner, said in the middle of the celebration. "This is it."

Lenny was named MVP of the game, completing 12 of 17 passes for 142 yards and the touchdown pass to me. It was fitting, not just because of his performance in the game, but because of all he endured during the previous five days.

"No, the gambling thing didn't give me any extra incentive," Lenny said to the reporters. "How could it? I approached this game as a big game, as an opportunity to be the best. You don't need outside motivation.

"Winning a game like this is a big thing, because if you win you don't have to explain anything. We've been explaining our Green Bay game for three years."

Lenny even received a phone call from President Nixon.

And so, while my teammates, coaches and quarterback were celebrating, I was shedding a few tears. I was so happy about winning—about becoming a champion—but I was especially happy for Lenny, for making it through all the bullshit and showing everybody who the number one quarterback on the number-one team really was.

9

THE "FIGHT"

There was one helluva parade waiting for us we when returned from New Orleans. The moment we touched down at Kansas City International Airport, ecstatic fans were everywhere along the 20-mile route to the city, and a huge throng of people lined the downtown streets as we wound our way to the Liberty Memorial for a victory rally. Even the cold weather couldn't chill our happiness and the fans' cheers. Gloster and I rode in one of the several open convertibles that carried the team, loving every second of the rowdy voices mixed with floating confetti in the frosty air. Police reports put the overall number of fans at around 175,00. It was sweet.

"This is the greatest football and sports town in the world," Lenny the Cool told the swelling crowd at the Memorial. "We are at the pinnacle."

It's too bad it didn't last longer.

As the defending world champs, the 1970 Kansas City Chiefs had a respectable season, but we were never able to find a rhythm within the season and sustain a consistency that would have propelled us back to the playoffs. We didn't play anywhere near the level we had played at the previous two years. I don't know if it was injuries or any one thing you can pinpoint as the reason. I do know we didn't have the fire we usually had. It was a nonchalant season. We played the games, let it go and didn't worry about it. It was the first season of the new NFL with two conferences, the AFC and NFC. I still think we had one of the better teams in the league, but if you don't play your best week after week, you can't win in the long run. And that was our problem that season.

Or maybe the Oakland Raiders were our biggest problem.

In many ways, 1970 mirrored 1967. The Chiefs were the team to beat, and everyone was gunning for us. We had targets on our jerseys—and got the best effort from every team we played. In previous years, that hadn't been a problem for us. And like the previous four years, if we could beat the Raiders, we would win the division.

When we reported to training camp, strike talk among the league's players was everywhere. A strike actually was called—a fact many people forget—at the end of July. Because we won the 1969 world championship, the Chiefs were scheduled to play the College All-Stars in Chicago on July 31. We weren't going to play because of the impending strike, but Stram told us that it was part of the deal as world champs; that it wasn't really an exhibition—we were going to get paychecks. The game was our reward for being the champs. We played and won easily, 24-3, but the strike started the next day. It lasted all of four days, and then everything returned to normal.

We played the Vikings the first week of the season in Minnesota, and they dominated us, winning easily 27-10. They played the way we played against them in New Orleans the previous January. It was a rotten way to start the season. The following week we made our debut on *Monday Night Football* and smoked the Colts, 44-22. But we lost at Denver and beat the Patriots and Bengals before losing to the Cowboys.

A major change on the team occurred on October 15 when the Chiefs traded Mike Garrett, the best of our running backs, to the

Chargers for a future draft pick. It was a move I didn't like at all—a move a lot of the other players didn't like. But Garrett wanted to leave; he supposedly didn't want to play football any more and had hinted he was going to try and play major-league baseball. Ed Podolak took over the top running back slot on the offense, and he was great. Ed didn't have the speed Garrett had, but he had the desire and was hungry for success. Even though we had played six up and down games in a sluggish fashion and had a 3-3 record, we were still very much in the division race.

And the Raiders were coming to town.

There was a lot of hate between the Chiefs and the Raiders at that point, but there was also respect. I think the news media built up the Raiders-Chiefs rivalry, and the fans really locked into it because the Raiders were the team that always kept the Chiefs from making

The Raiders' defensive backs, in this case Nemiah Wilson and Dave Grayson, always hit me hard. (Photo provided by the Kansas Collection, U. of Kansas Archives)

the playoffs. There was a reason for that: They were a very good team with a nucleus of great ballplayers.

The game with Oakland was crucial to us. The Raiders came into the contest with a 3-2-1 record, and the Broncos were 4-2. A win would keep us near the top of the division and also put us ahead of the Raiders. Staying ahead of the Silver and Black was imperative.

The game started slowly as we tried to run the ball, and the Raiders did the same. Early in the second quarter, Lenny hit me on a 56-yard pass—the Raiders' cornerback barely tripped me up to keep me out of the end zone—and we had a first and goal at the four-yard line. Wendell Hayes scored to put us up, 7-0. The Raiders scored two touchdowns, and Stenerud kicked a 33-yard field goal to make the score Raiders 14, Chiefs 10 going into the fourth quarter.

With less than 12 minutes remaining in the game, Lenny led us on an 85-yard drive that was culminated by his 13-yard pass to me for the go-ahead touchdown. The score was 17-14. When we got the ball back with 4:41 remaining in the game, we tried to run out the clock. After collecting a couple of first downs, Lenny brought us to the line for a third and nine at the Raiders' 48-yard line. There was 1:08 left in the game.

What happened next would become the most infamous play of my career.

Lenny took the snap, faked a handoff to his left, then spun around and ran a beautiful bootleg up the right side of the field, gaining 19 yards before he was finally tripped up and stopped. Lenny ended up face down, curled up on the turf. And then Ben Davidson, the Raiders' huge, ugly, mustachioed lineman came lumbering from behind and dove into Lenny's back, as vicious and flagrant a late hit as I've ever seen. Davidson somersaulted over Lenny after the spear. I was running up from behind the play, ready to congratulate Lenny, when I saw the hit. As Davidson popped up to his feet, I was right there.

And my protective nature—plus a lot of rage—took over.

I grabbed Davidson by the neck, twisted and slammed him to the ground. It looked powerful, almost like a good wrestling hold. I only had to hold him for a second because I knew my teammates would be there in a flash, and they were. Both benches emptied and the two teams shoved and pushed each other, pulling Davidson and me apart. It took more than five minutes to restore order.

> *"The bond that was formed helped [the Chiefs] feel like a family. That was particularly evident in the 1970 game against our biggest rivals, the Oakland Raiders. With a minute left in the game, Ben Davidson lunged and speared me after I picked up a first down. He was tagged with the unnecessary roughness penalty, but he also got tagged by something else...or, I should say, someone else. Almost immediately, Otis went after Davidson. I have to admit that I wasn't surprised when Otis did that, because he was that type of player. He was protecting me. Looking back, I wish that he hadn't done it, because he was ejected. We ultimately didn't win the game, and it cost us the division championship, but Otis was watching out for a member of his 'family.' It also didn't surprise me that once Otis jumped on Davidson, the rest of our teammates jumped in there, too."*
>
> —Len Dawson

• • •

> *"What happened is that Lenny went down and Ben Davidson, who had a reputation of always hitting late, drilled Lenny. He speared him right in the back. Otis jumped on Davidson and then all hell broke loose. Everyone from the benches ran out, and that was from the other side of the field. It was just a melee with everybody hitting each other. We all backed Otis up. Davidson always had that reputa-*

tion of spearing somebody or hitting late, especially when he was trying to get the quarterback out of the game, and that's what he did. Dawson was Otis's bread and butter, so he was going to protect him— I thought Otis was more than justified with his actions. We never loved the Oakland Raiders anyway. They were definitely our top and most hated rival."

—Ed Budde

•••

"Otis took Ben Davidson down in 1970 after Davidson had hit Lenny late on the play. Otis just ran over and grabbed ahold of Ben Davidson, picked him up in the air and body slammed him. And that started one of the memorable fights with the Oakland Raiders—first Ben spearing Lenny and then Otis making a fool out of Ben Davidson."

—Ed Podolak

Penalty flags littered the field. This was the outcome: Davidson was penalized 15 yards, which moved the ball to the Raiders' 14-yard line, and I was ejected from the game. But the Raiders argued that if I was thrown out, the

The Raiders' Ben Davidson was big, bad and ugly. (Photo provided by the Kansas City Chiefs)

Chiefs should also be penalized. After a long discussion, the refs agreed and refused to give us the important first down. They called it a continuous-play penalty, and the rules stipulated that the down must be replayed—offsetting fouls. Coach Stram countered that if Davidson was guilty of piling on, as he was called for, then the play was already over. No dice. The ball was moved back to the original line of scrimmage (actually one yard farther back; the officials messed that up, too) and we had to replay the down.

"I didn't think the quarterback had been tackled," Davidson reasoned about the play following the game. "I was touching him down to make sure he didn't get up and run." You could hear his sarcastic tone and see the twinkle in his eyes as he said that. Years later, Davidson gave a truthful account of his action at the end of the play in the book *Raiders Forever*: "We needed a touchdown to win and field goal to tie, so when Lenny rolled out, he tripped over a leg, and I figured if I could hurt him, we'd be back in first place next week, so I speared him and did a somersault over him."

Podolak gained three yards on the replayed down, and then Jerrel Wilson punted the ball out of the end zone. The Raiders were on their own 20 with two timeouts and less than a minute to play. And even then, we still should have won. After Oakland's Fred Biletnikoff caught a pass and was downed at our 47-yard line, the Raiders were out of timeouts. But the clock was stopped because Jim Kearney was injured on the play.

Two plays later, the Raiders' old man, George Blanda, eked a 48-yard field goal over the crossbar and Oakland tied the score, 17-17, with three seconds remaining. And we still weren't done, because the Chiefs' Jerry Mays, our defensive end, drew two 15-yard penalties for arguing with the officials and Oakland kicked off from our 30-yard line. Their onside kick was covered by Podolak, and the game was finally over—a tie.

"I remember the game in 1970 when we had the Raiders beat-the one where Ben Davidson hit Dawson. That stands out in my mind. We probably would have gone back to the Super Bowl if we had won that game. You know, the Raiders and the Chiefs had no love. The Chiefs didn't like the Raiders when I came to Kansas City, and the Raiders didn't like the Chiefs. That's the way it was. When we played, I remember it was very intense, a real rivalry. What's in my mind about that game? If that [spearing] hadn't happened, who knows, instead of one Super Bowl, we might have won two or three Super Bowls. If you go back and take that year—1970—and the following year when Miami beat us in overtime, we could have won the Super Bowl three years in a row."

—Jim Marsalis

•••

"It had to do with the character of the Chiefs' players—If you hit one, you might as well hit everybody. On the field, we took care of each other, and that was it. I talk to Ben Davidson, see him all the time. I do a lot of stuff with him, and he's a great guy. On the field, it was a different story. I'll bet Otis didn't know that was Ben Davidson he went after. To him, 'the guy who was wearing that Raiders jersey did something wrong.' Otis was the closest one to Davidson and Dawson, and when it happened, he felt it first. Then he slammed him and everybody else just followed through and joined the fighting."

—Bobby Bell

After the game, Stram stormed into the officials' locker room, unloaded a barrage of expletives and anger on the officials, and then

In the home game against the Raiders in 1970, I cost our team a victory by protecting Len Dawson late in the fourth quarter. (Photos courtesy of the Taylor Family Collection)

1. Lenny is tripped after making a big gain on a scramble that was going to give the Chiefs a first down.

2. The Raiders Ben Davidson speared Lenny in the back after he was already down.

3. Incensed, I immediately grabbed Davidson...

4. ... and wrestled him to the ground. A big melee started—both benches ran onto the field—and I was eventually thrown out of the game, the Chiefs were penalized, and the Raiders came back to tie the game in the final seconds.

returned to our clubhouse. It was very uncharacteristic of our coach, but we had been screwed by the officials.

"I've never been more proud of a 40-man squad," Stram said after the game. "They played with great effort and purpose. It's just a shame they were deprived of an opportunity to win the football game. It's an emotional game. You fight for your lives. It's team play. And I think it's what wins it for you in the end."

What did a tie game mean to us? Denver had lost that day, so the Raiders moved into first place while we dropped to third. A win would have put us into a tie for first and Oakland would have been in third place.

What happened is what happened, and I guess you could make the argument that my retaliation on Davidson cost us the game. In fact, I've always blamed myself for the tie, because there were many losses we endured as a team that never felt as bad as that tie. But I would have hit the guy no matter what team it was, because I was doing it for Lenny. I had no idea I was going to be fined (I think it was $500), but I was doing it for Lenny because he was my teammate, my quarterback. My other teammates never got on my back about the play, and I was respected more for doing what I did than some of the guys who stood back and said of Davidson, "I can't believe he did that." I reacted forcibly—maybe I overreacted.

Playing the Oakland Raiders was hell—it was never easy against them. The fight we had at the game that day, it wasn't just a push-and-shove type of thing. I went after Davidson with all my might.

Through the years I've seen Davidson a lot, at least once a year at banquet or some other function. I was in Cleveland a couple of years ago, and he was sitting at a table, talking to a bunch of old players. I snuck up behind him and grabbed his neck. It really scared the hell out of him at first, but he laughed when he looked back and saw who I was.

"The Riddler" (Frank Pitts, No. 25), "Big O" (me, No. 89), and "Rat Hair," (Gloster Richardson, No. 30), the three Chiefs receivers from the SWAC. (Photo provided by **The Topeka C-J***)*

"Coach Stram instituted the idea about the team being together the night before a game. And the reason for that is he wanted everybody to be on the same page. No wives, girlfriends, nobody but us at the hotel. That's how we started going over to Overland Park, and while we were there, he would have a band or something come out and Wendell Hayes would take the mike and start singing. We'd have a meeting, eat, and go to bed. Sometimes we would have the wives come out, too, but they would have to go home and we would stay and be together. During training camp, we'd have a day where we would have all the wives and family there, and we'd still have to stay and everybody would have to go back home. I think he pushed that because he said that we had to win as a team if we wanted to win. And that brought us together. After that, you just couldn't break us away from each other. It was a good time because back then it wasn't as fast as it is now and everybody wanted to talk and be around with

the other guys. Especially Otis. He always wanted to sit under the goal posts and talk instead of running to take a shower."

—Frank Pitts

The rest of the season was filled with the same inconsistency, even though we won four of our next five games. We beat Houston and Pittsburgh, but tied St. Louis. Then we beat San Diego and avenged our loss to the Broncos. When we traveled to Oakland for the next to last game of the year, the Western Division title was once again on the line. We played a sloppy, conservative game and the Raiders defeated us easily, 20-6. We lost to the Chargers in a meaningless game to end the season with a 7-5-2 record.

My personal performance in 1970 was poor. I caught just 34 passes and scored only three touchdowns. My best game had been against the Raiders in the 17-all tie—I caught four passes for 129 yards and a TD. Our offensive production overall was way down from the year before. But the Chiefs had always been resilient in the past. I knew we still had the stuff to become champions again, and I knew I was still capable of being one of the top receivers in the NFL.

10

ALL I WANT FOR CHRISTMAS . . .

It is the memory that lingers forever—the frozen moment in time that wraps itself around your heart and won't let go. As Miami's little Garo Yepremian positioned himself for a game-winning field goal attempt after more than 82 excruciating and exciting minutes of hard-fought football, I stood on the sideline feeling powerless because I couldn't stop him and feeble because I hadn't done more to help my team win the game. When Yepremian stepped into the kick and the ball sailed through the uprights to give the Dolphins a 27-24 win, a permanent shroud of loss and regret fell over me.

The Kansas City Chiefs' high-powered 1971 season of success, and my own year of personal excellence, was over. We weren't going to return to the Super Bowl, we weren't going to be champions.

Christmas Day would never be the same for me again.

•••

The 1971 Kansas City Chiefs were an awesome group of individuals, but more importantly, we were a cohesive, tight-knit team. The veteran players knew each other well, and we played like it. Coach

Stram had instilled the family atmosphere within his system, and we thrived under his coaching structure. Personally, I was ready to bust loose. I'd had three subpar seasons—by my standards—in a row and I was anxious to reestablish myself.

The organization went through a few changes before the year started. Gloster Richardson and Frank Pitts were both gone—traded away. Elmo Wright, a brilliantly talented rookie from the University of Houston, stepped into the other starting receiver spot. Three key players from our previous championship teams, Fred Arbanas, E. J. Holub and Jerry Mays, had retired. Stram kept our running game a top priority—Ed Podolak was masterful at finding open holes and slashing for yardage—but we were going to pass the ball more than we had in previous years.

Just how good were the Chiefs that year? By season's end, no fewer than 11 Chiefs would be named to the Pro Bowl, including myself. We were dominant on both sides of the ball, with experienced veterans at almost every key position. And we had balance—a strong running attack, excellent passing, a good defensive pass rush, a tremendous trio of linebackers and the best secondary in the NFL. In short, when training camp broke and the regular season was upon us, I was positive we were going to return to the top of the league.

But the craziest thing happened...we lost our first game. We opened at San Diego, and after leading 14-0 at the half, we fell asleep and let them come back to defeat us, 21-14. The Oilers put a scare into us the following week, but we held on for our first win of the year, 20-16, and stopped the Broncos in Denver the following week, 16-3. The Chargers came to Kansas City for our home opener, and we avenged the earlier loss with a 31-10 win.

Pittsburgh came to Municipal for a *Monday Night Football* game, and I had one of the best games of my career, catching six passes for 190 yards and two touchdowns. And since my mother was at the game, that really made the evening special as we rocked the Steelers,

Another one-handed catch, this one against Buffalo in 1971. (Photo provided by AP/WWP)

38-16. I paid homage to our offensive line after the game for the excellent protection they afforded Lenny. You can't throw long if the quarterback is harassed, and they gave Lenny and me the time we needed to complete the plays.

The undefeated Washington Redskins came calling the following week. We started poorly in the game and fell behind 17-6 at the half. But Lenny led us back, hitting me and then Elmo with a couple of TD passes to pull us even, 20-20. Late in the fourth quarter, we had the ball deep in our own territory and faced a third and 18. Lenny hit me on a short pass, and I dragged a few Redskin defenders the final seven or eight yards and made it past the marker for a first down. We continued to move down the field, and from the Washington 28, Lenny called my number for the end zone. He got hit as he released the ball, and as I crossed the goal line and went up for the ball, the Redskins' Pat Fischer jumped on my back and pinned my right arm to my side. I reached up and pulled the ball in with my left hand and scored the game-winning touchdown.

All those times I'd pissed off Coach Stram for practicing one-handed catches had paid off.

> *"I remember a couple of plays in 1971 against the Washington Redskins—they were undefeated, and we'd only lost once. Needless to say, it was a tough, close game. We had a third and long situation with Otis in the slot, and my primary target on the play was Elmo Wright. As it turned out, Elmo was not open, nor was anybody else. On a last-ditch effort, I threw the ball out to Otis, who hadn't moved far off the line of scrimmage. Not only did he make the catch, but he also broke three or four tackles to pick up the first down and keep the drive alive. Later in that drive was the famous catch where Washington's Pat Fischer practically had one of Otis's arms tied to his side, but Otis reached up and hauled in the pass with his free hand for a touchdown. I will never forget those two plays, and to think*

they were from just one particular drive! Those are great illustrations of the type of raw ability [Otis] had."

—Len Dawson

The next game was at Oakland, and we led 20-17 late in the fourth quarter. The Raiders drove all the way to our one-yard line in the final minute, but on fourth down they opted for the game-tying field goal instead of going for the win. I think we caught a break, because I was certain they'd go in for the touchdown and beat us. A mediocre Jets team beat us the next week in New York, 13-10, and on Thanksgiving we lost to the Lions in Detroit, 32-21. After we put away the 49ers on *Monday Night Football*, the Raiders came to Municipal for a game that once again would decide the Western Division title. A loss in the game would also eliminate us from the wild-card playoff spot.

Like so many Raiders-Chiefs games in the past, it appeared we were once again going to outplay our number-one foe but still lose. We controlled the game throughout, yet the Raiders scored a fourth-quarter touchdown to go ahead, 14-13. But 1971 wasn't like previous seasons. Facing a third and long inside our own 20-yard line late in the game, Lenny gave me a simple command in the huddle.

"Get open."

I found a little seam in the Raiders' coverage, pulled in Lenny's pass and picked up the first down. He threw to me three more times on that drive, and on his fourth pass to me I was tripped as the ball approached me—pass interference. I would have caught it and scored. As it was, we ran the ball three times and Stenerud kicked the division-winning field goal.

"I remember in '71, it was the final time we played Oakland in Municipal Stadium and we were behind with about 8-10 yards to

go to get a much-needed first down. The winner of the game would win the division and go to the playoffs. It was third down, and we were in the shadow of our own goalposts. Leonard looked at Otis in the huddle and said, 'Get open.' Otis squared in, caught the pass, ran over a couple people, and made the first down. Leonard kept throwing to him, got us out of our own territory and we went on down the field to score, and that was the victory that won the division."

—Ed Podolak

The '71 season was also the last year we played at Municipal Stadium. I loved that old stadium and the surrounding neighborhood as well. It gave us a definite home-field advantage. Built as a baseball stadium, a large set of movable bleachers were placed from the left field line over to center field for our games, which cut off a good portion of the outfield of the baseball layout and formed the rectangular football field. Because the front row of seats that extended from the right field foul pole to where home plate was were virtually at field level, both benches for the football teams during a game were on the same side of the field, in front of the bleachers. We didn't mind being that close to the opposing teams, but I know most of our opponents didn't like it.

The stadium was pretty old—almost 50 years in 1971—and it gave us a real blue-collar mentality. The fans were close to us, and there was an old scoreboard hovering high over the playing surface from the center field part of the stadium. When the place was sold out, our fans were incredibly loud, producing thunderous and piercing tones. We loved it.

"Otis was such a talented performer, catching the ball with ease and making so many big plays. You'd say to yourself, 'How in the world did he catch that ball?' And, of course, once he caught the ball, he

had such great speed that very rarely did he ever get caught. Otis was a big-play guy and very instrumental in the success we had in Kansas City, especially in 1971. When I look back, we probably we didn't get the ball to him as much as we should have as a receiver at that particular stage of our history and growth. But I felt very strongly about the balance part of the game. We had good running backs. We had great offensive linemen. We had to make sure we diversified what we were doing and to make sure that we did a variety of things instead of overdoing one thing. We wanted to get the ball to him as often as we possibly could. He was very, very special. He took a lot of pride in catching and running the ball and making touchdowns and that kind of thing. He was terrific, just a fantastic player."

—Hank Stram

The weather was unusually mild and pleasant on Christmas Day in 1971-59 degrees—when we lined up against the Miami Dolphins for the first-ever playoff game in Kansas City. The Dolphins were the Eastern Division champs of the AFC and had very good players on both sides of the ball. Bob Griese was an excellent quarterback, Paul Warfield one of the best receivers in the game, and fullback Larry Czonka was a veritable battering ram when he ran the ball. On defense, the Dolphins were led by middle linebacker Nick Buoniconti, defensive tackle Manny Fernandez, and safety Jake Scott. They were solid and just a year away from going undefeated in the NFL.

In our very first offensive series, what the Dolphins were trying to do became obvious. Every time I came off the line I was double- or triple-teamed. They guarded me that way the entire game, and I found there was very little I could do. But that's not an excuse; I should have been able to get open more than I did.

But we still had offensive success. Stenerud booted a field goal early in the first quarter, and Podolak scored a touchdown on a seven-yard pass from Lenny. The Dolphins scored their first TD early in the second quarter, and Lenny tried to hit me in with a pass late in the first half. It was intercepted, which set up a field goal for the Dolphins, tying the score, 10-10, at the half. My inability to shake the Dolphins' double- and triple-team pass coverage opened up the other areas of our offense. Ed Podolak began to make slashing runs all over the field—on sweeps, kick returns, and screen passes.

We had lost a great opportunity to score a touchdown midway through the second quarter when Stram called for a fake field goal. Stenerud would take a direct snap and run with the ball. With two blockers in front of him, it would have been an easy touchdown. But either long-snapper Bobby Bell didn't think Stenerud was ready for the ball or he thought the fake had been audibled off. I'm not sure what he thought, and maybe he doesn't know, either. Instead of snapping the ball to Jan, he rifled it to Dawson, the holder. Improvising as best he could, Stenerud kicked the ball and just missed the field goal.

Early in the second half, Lenny was able to throw to me three consecutive times, the only receptions I made in the game. The first catch, for six yards, gave us a first down. The next was for three yards, and the third catch was for another three yards, but after I caught the ball I lateraled to Ed, who then ran for an additional 16 yards. A clipping penalty cut the overall gain on that play to four yards. We sustained the drive, however, and eight plays later Jim Otis ran in from a yard out to put us back in the lead, 17-10. There were just over five minutes remaining in the third quarter.

Miami came right back and tied the score at the end of the third quarter. A beautiful 63-yard pass play from Lenny to Elmo Wright put the ball on the Dolphins' three-yard line midway through the last period, and Podolak scored on the next play. Miami then put together a nine-play drive and tied the score once again with 1:42 left in the fourth quarter.

Podolak followed with the play of the game and what should have been the play of his life. He took the kickoff, ran straight up the middle of the field, veered to his left and flew down the sideline before being pushed out at the Miami 22-yard line. We went crazy on the sideline, thinking a field goal from Stenerud would be automatic and win the game. We ran the ball three times and Jan trotted onto the field. Emmitt Thomas came over to me just before Stenerud's field-goal attempt.

"He's going to miss it," he said. "We're going to go to overtime."

The kick was wide right.

And Stenerud had a field-goal attempt blocked on our first possession of overtime. The two teams slugged back and forth against one another after that, and when Czonka busted a 29-yard run midway through the second overtime period, Miami was in position to win the game. Yepremian's 37-yard kick was true, sucking the life out of our season as it sailed through the uprights.

"In 1971, we had the best team we ever had. We had a better team than we had the year we won the Super Bowl. Going into the playoff game [with Miami] we had no doubt. We knew the Dolphins had a good team, but we had such good camaraderie and team chemistry that we felt like we could beat anybody. When Stenerud missed the field goal, everybody blamed him. But Stenerud wasn't the reason we lost the game, because he had kicked so many field goals to help us win during the regular season. That made me feel real bad. Marv Fleming, a tight end on the Dolphins, caught a five-yard touchdown pass, and he was my responsibility. I put a comment in the paper that if he hadn't have caught that little pass, then we would have won. It wasn't Stenerud's fault we lost, and you have to give Miami credit. They had a good game plan, but we pretty well shut them down. I

think the defense played well and the offense played well. There were two good teams playing and unfortunately, it goes into double overtime, and one of them has to lose on a field goal. I think we had the best team—the best team did not win that game. If we had won that game right there, we would have two Super Bowl rings instead of one."

—Jim Kearney

Ed Podolak—who had been spectacular, gaining 350 yards of total offense and scoring two TDs—cried in the locker room after the game. Curley Culp slammed his helmet into several walls. Stenerud sat in shock as he answered reporters' questions. Hank Stram fought to maintain control over his emotions.

"It's a shame to fight that hard, play that well, and not win," Stram said following the game. "But it boils down to kicks. They made theirs. We didn't. We got a super return from Ed Podolak and we had our chance to put the game away. We didn't do it."

"I have the worst feeling anyone could have," Stenerud said. "I have no idea what I'm going to do now. I feel like hiding, I don't feel like playing football. It's a shame guys play like hell, like our team did, and lose because of a missed field goal. It's unbearable. It's totally unbearable."

I was also in shock and angry because I didn't contribute to the offense. I hadn't been able to make a big play that might have won the game either before or during the overtime.

"I think at that time Lenny was pretty much in charge of the plays for the offense. He and Coach Stram had identified the fact that Miami was trying to take Otis out of the game, and by doing that it certainly gave more opportunities to the run the ball. I will never forget one play that was called in that game where we finally got the ball to Otis

Trying to stay warm, while I reflect on the progress of a game during the 1971 season. (Photo courtesy of the Taylor Family Collection)

and I was behind him as he was being tackled. He lateraled the ball to me and I gained about another 20 yards, but the referees brought it back, calling clipping on the play. Still, it was Otis making a big play out of what was just a regular play for other athletes. He always had a knack for doing that."

—Ed Podolak

"Any time you don't accomplish a goal, someone is going to say there was something wrong. When we played Miami in the longest game ever, we should have won that ballgame. It should never have gone into the sixth quarter. We had three chances to win it and we didn't. And then the tide turned. You get the opportunities and you've got to make the best of them. We had them, but we didn't take advantage of the opportunities and lost. I think the better football team didn't win that game. I also think the 1971 Chiefs were the best team I played on offensively and defensively. The 1969 team—we were a super defensive team. Who knows…if we would have gotten back to the Super Bowl, we might have won it two more times."

—Jim Marsalis

•••

"I thought we would never end the game. It was like two games in one, and I think it was one of the hardest-hitting games we ever played in. Every time I turned around, here came Larry Czonka. If I had to pick a tough back, I'd pick him because every time I hit him, I hit him with everything I had. The next thing I know, he gets up and here he comes back again. I remember hitting him a couple times, and I got up and my helmet was across my face and I'm looking through the ear hole. I'm going, 'Man, take that.' And this guy was wobbling around back there and still they give the ball to him again. He must have carried the ball 30-some times in that game. That was a game, I tell you what; it just went up and down the field. We thought we had the game won a couple of times on a field goal and we missed them. And they thought they had it won. And the next thing you know, we're tied again. After the game, I remember going to the locker room, and two hours later I was still in there. I walked into the shower with my uniform on. I just could not move.

Every bone, every muscle in my body was stiff. I think it was one of the greatest games we ever played in. Our offense kept moving the ball; they just couldn't get the touchdown like they were supposed to."

—Bobby Bell

•••

"The longest game in history against Miami—let me tell you how ironic that was. I got traded from Kansas City to the Cowboys that year, so I was in Dallas. We had played and won our playoff game, and were in the clubhouse, watching the Chiefs and Dolphins. I'm saying, 'Come on, Chiefs.' And some of the guys on the Cowboys were saying, 'No, we don't want the Chiefs if we want to win. We want Miami in the Super Bowl.' The Dolphins hadn't been to the Super Bowl before, and when we played them, we ended up winning the game. But I know the Cowboys couldn't have beaten the Chiefs that year, not with the team Dallas had."

—Gloster Richardson

Why did we lose? I think we were thinking ahead—in a sensible way—that we would win the game. And we were ready to play Miami. What really turned the game in our favor was that Ed had such a great day, even though that took us away from what we really wanted to do on offense. He was so good in that game that it was worth changing the game plan, so we didn't throw the ball that much. All season long we were a play-action, reverse and sweep-type team. Our main pass patterns were short, quick-outs, square-ins and slant-ins. But Miami very effectively took those away from us the entire game, and Ed was able to take advantage, running the ball and catching short screen passes.

When we lost to the Dolphins on Christmas Day, I believe in my heart that it marked the beginning of the demise the Chiefs organization. We had matured so much, had learned to play together so well as a team, and had learned how to come from behind—something Chiefs teams in the past had had problems doing. Our regular season was worthy of a championship; we had numerous big plays during the year, and people across the country were recognizing the Chiefs, finally, as one of the top teams in pro football. Think about how many lives were changed from that one game. Right now, more than 30 years later, I still wake up on Christmas morning with the same thing on my mind—losing that game. I've asked all my teammates and they say the same thing happens to them. Amazing how one event could make such a difference. And on the flip side, I'm sure all the Dolphins' players from that season wake up on Christmas morning smiling, feeling good about the memories of the game.

I still don't have a reasonable explanation for why we lost that game. I had a hard time dealing with it then, have a hard time with it today, and I'll have a hard time with it tomorrow. I know we lost the game, but still I play it over and over again in my mind. The bad part is that the more you play it back, the more times we lose. Sometimes you want to go back and make it so the Chiefs win, but we still lose—again and again and again.

I have never watched the film of that game, and I never will.

11

THE OLD PRO

Nothing lasts forever.

My final three-plus seasons with the Chiefs were somewhat productive, but the injuries I'd endured over the past 10 years had slowed me a little—and I felt it. The little nagging things—sore muscles, ankle tweaks, tender ribs—weren't as easy to shake off. I'd also sustained a great deal of damage to my knees.

Man, it's hell to get old.

There was a very weird thing about the injuries I suffered throughout my career—I bet 99 percent of them were on the left side of my body. It always perplexed me, because every problem I had, specifically the groin muscle pull and knee problems, happened on the left side of my body. How or why that happened, I have no idea. I was never a weakling when it came to injuries, and I was pretty stout in my aggressiveness to play through the pain. I've never tried to slough off because of them or rest when I could have played. I saw some guys really use and play injuries for all they were worth. I couldn't stand the guys who did that. They made me sick. But maybe they had more sense than I had, protecting themselves for longer careers.

I had problems with my knee all the way through my career. People can't know the pain and suffering it caused. Even when I got to college—I had my first knee injury in high school, in the 10th grade, and they didn't know if it would get well enough for me to go to college—a lot of guys told me that I wasn't going to get drafted. But I always seemed to be able to play through the pain. I think I would have gotten drafted much higher if I didn't have the bad knee. When I was drafted by the Chiefs, they were worried about that.

One of the worst injuries I had—of the ones that caused me to miss games—was when I was coming across the middle of the field, caught a pass and had my face mask smashed into my face in the process. I was hit smack in the face with a helmet. My face mask—I always wore two single bars so I could see the entire field—crumpled and stuck into my lower jaw. It went into my mouth under my tongue. I walked off the field with a helmet stuck into me like that. I remember my mother asking afterwards if I was hurt. Hell, the damn bar shot straight through my gums!

I had a few surgeries on my knee while I was with the Chiefs. The doctor would look at me, grin and just start cutting, like he was slicing a steak or something. We had one doctor whom I thought was a butcher, and I had a couple of operations from him over the course of my years with the team. He didn't do much of a job. But then we were very fortunate to have Dr. Howard Ellfeldt become the team doctor. Dr. Ellfeldt was instrumental in helping several different players' injuries. He didn't feed us any lines and actually suggested that I quit playing because my knees had gotten so bad, especially if I wanted to be walking when I was 50.

We couldn't even talk about being sore because Hank would run us off if we complained. But when I played, I ran over people, and I was so sore sometimes I couldn't get out of bed to go to the bathroom. On Monday mornings I got into the whirlpool to try to ease the soreness. By the middle of the week, I was usually close to 100 percent again.

Before each game, season after season, I would put my left shoe on first, tie it up and tape it up. Then I'd put my right shoe on and tape it up. I always taped my ankles and shoes by myself. I had a knee brace, too. The worst pain I've been through was with my knee, and it was not worth it. For two years, Dr. Ellfeldt would numb my knee and stick a needle in, and the trainer would hold it in place. That would suck out the fluids, and I could see the knee shrink up as they did that. Then he'd take out another needle and shoot me up to kill the pain. I cried like a baby because it hurt so bad. And I had to have that done every week. I used to bite through a dry towel just to handle the pain. I had to be at the training room at 11:00 am for a 3:00 pm game. I always went at least two hours early because I didn't want anyone to see me go through that pain.

Of all the things that I did and had happen to me in football, if I had to do one thing over, I would have worked out a little harder in the off season. There's no doubt that I would have benefited from the off-season programs they have today, and because of the equipment that they have now, I probably would have been a much better and stronger football player.

•••

There's a fine art to catching a football. A receiver has to have talent, ability, a feel for the ball, and knowledge about the way the game works. I also think a receiver needs to be instinctive. I never would have made it if I hadn't let my instincts take over on almost every play. I once said during my career that if you woke me up in the middle of the night and threw a football at me, I'd catch it. That's instinct. As much as I honed and perfected every aspect of my talent, I also worked at letting my instinct kick in—just letting things happen, making the moves and sticking it to the defensive back.

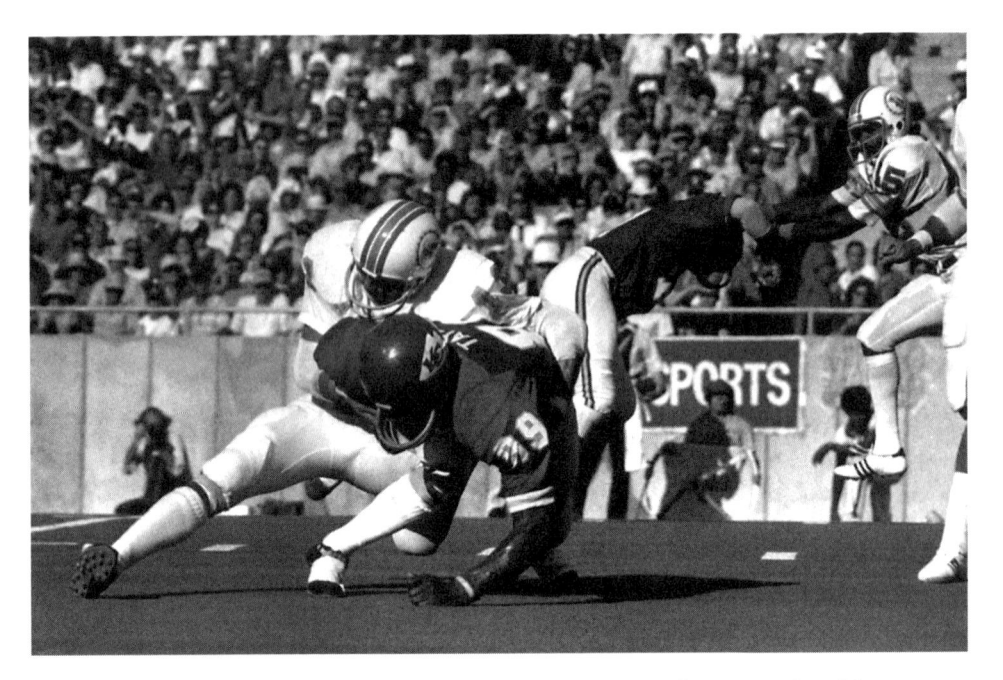

I'm about to be smashed into the unforgiving AstroTurf at Arrowhead by a Dolphins defensive back. (Photo provided by the Kansas Collection, U. of Kansas Archives)

I never had a favorite pattern or specific play that I liked best. The curls, square-outs, ups, posts—they were all good for me. I did, on occasion, come back to the huddle and suggest a particular route or play, but that was strictly in a specific game situation we might have been in, or maybe I'd found a weakness in the man covering me. All the routes took precision timing and good footwork. It's one thing to know where you're supposed to go; it's another to get there.

Something I learned early in my career was to punish the guy covering me. What I mean is this: When I caught the ball, I wanted the defensive back to pay a price when he tried to bring me down. I'd protect myself with my shoulders or elbows. Maybe I was a little mean and nasty at times, but that temperament took me to the top of my game. Mindset is just as important—maybe more so—than being in perfect physical condition. If you don't think while playing the game, you'll lose.

"Catching the ball is perfunctory. It's what you do with the ball once you get it. Otis exploded when he got the ball. It was like putting a bullet in a gun when he received it. I think that was the critical thing. He was a very gifted player with a lot of talent and a big heart—he was an executor. You could depend on him—rely on him to make a play. Everybody knew that. It's that chemistry thing—that bond. Everybody knew it on the team. Everybody knew it in the organization. Everybody knew it in the stands."

—Curtis McClinton

I was a hands and fingers receiver. What I mean by that is I always tried to catch the ball with my fingers. And to catch the ball, you have to see it. As I stated earlier, I always wore two single bars for my face mask—I didn't want the distraction of extra items in front of my eyes. Like a windshield wiper is a distraction. Now imagine a hand and think of a football. Your eyes pick up the tip—the first part of the football—and you slow it down by the tip. The center of the ball is the body and the end is the brakes. If you don't catch it on the brakes, it's gone—on the ground. You have to look at the tip of the ball as it comes to you. That's what I tell the guys when they run to the sidelines, holding their hands out in front of them instead of waiting until the ball gets there to put up their hands. Imagine an airplane as it is leveling off. The flaps go up or down; it goes this way with the rudder or it can glide. It is the same thing with your body. If you have your arms up and your head looking another direction, you're going to float in that direction. When I saw the ball, I didn't prepare myself to catch until it got to me. And they are not teaching that today as far as I can tell when I go to games and watch them on television. Also, if you put your hands out you'll break your speed. The last three yards before a ball comes in is the best—and, I think, the only—time to make a catch.

I'm always asked what I consider to be the best catch I ever made. I think the 46-yard TD play against the Vikings in Super Bowl IV is the best play I ever made, but the catch itself was pretty routine. My catch in the 1969 AFL championship game against Oakland that season pulled us out of the shadow of our own goal line and is a play I'm proud of because it set us up for the go-ahead score. I'm proud of the one-handed catch against Washington in 1971, not so much for the catch itself, but for the fact it was the game-winning touchdown. The thing all these receptions have in common is simple: I helped my team win.

•••

I was blessed to know and play with many, many great players—great men—while I was a member of the Kansas City Chiefs. I played with a superb quarterback, Lenny Dawson, but almost everybody else on our offense in my 11 seasons with the team was an excellent player, too. The respect and mutual admiration the Chiefs players had for one another throughout most of my career was one of the most significant factors in the team's overall accomplishments. As an individual, I know the guys I played with helped to make me a better player.

Frank Pitts. Frank was "The Riddler," and I mean just like the real Riddler, right out of the Batman TV show. What a laugh he had; what an obnoxious cackle! Something could be way out of sight, absolutely not funny at all, and Pitts would start laughing. Fifty guys could have heard what he heard, and all 50 guys would know that whatever happened or was said wasn't funny. But Frank would be laughing that Riddler laugh.

Early in his career we called him "Oops" because he dropped so many passes. He made significant improvement over the years, however, and became a dangerous receiver for the Chiefs. And man could he run—it came easy for him. He loved to run. Coach Stram would line us up for sprints after practice, and we would run 10 sets of 100-yard sprints, many times a lot more than that. The whistle would blow to start running and boom, Frank is 30 yards out in front of everybody, and he's laughing. We're pissed, telling him to slow down, and still he's laughing—still 30 yards ahead on each sprint. He was probably the fastest guy on the team, but he could be beat in the 40. Nobody, however, could beat him in the 100.

Frank and I both ran the reverse play for the Chiefs—51 pop g-o reverse and 52 pop g-o reverse (even numbers to the right and odd to the left). We would both run the reverse three to five times a season. In Super Bowl IV, Frank got the call three times because of the Vikings' defensive sets, and he was spectacular.

Gloster Richardson. Gloster and I were roommates for pretty much the whole time we were on the team together, and we're still close buddies today. The perfect scenario, as far as I was concerned, would have been for me to move to tight end, and Frank and Gloster would have been the wide outs. I don't think there was a secondary in either the AFL or the NFL that could have covered the three of us all at the same time. Gloster had the softest, sweetest hands you ever you wanted to see. We did get to play this scheme a few times, but never on a regular basis.

Gloster never seemed to get as much playing time as I did. The thing is, I wanted to win—which meant I wanted to play all the time. I wanted it with all my heart. And the guy I competed with for the number-one receiver job was also the guy I broke bread with and was great friends with—Gloster. I worked hard to get it. We were two soldiers fighting for the same job, and both of us wanted to be number one.

Today we laugh and cry about different aspects of life and talk about football and what it meant to us then and now. Gloster loves clothes, too, much like I do. He's a great golfer and has a sweet swing. I think—and this no stretch of my imagination—that Gloster could have been a great pro golfer.

Chris Burford. Chris was my mentor at wide receiver. When I first joined the Chiefs, a lot of guys kept me at arm's length, and you would have expected the other receivers to keep me at bay as well. I wasn't very disciplined when I became a pro because we didn't have a specific receivers coach at Prairie View, and I was used to doing things on my own. I was rough around the edges. But Burford, as well as Frank Jackson, took me under his wing and helped me a great deal—running six-yard patterns, driving the back out and closing on the guy.

Burford was the definition of slow motion; he had no speed at all. But he ran his routes to perfection, and I mean literally to perfection. He's a lawyer now, of course. He was always extremely smart. And he's always embarrassed when I say how much he helped me become a better receiver and claims that he didn't do anything, really. But he did, and he was there, helping and answering my questions. He taught me how to run a route.

Elmo Wright. He was supposed to be my protégé; Elmo was actually drafted by the Chiefs to replace me. He's probably the best example I know of a player who was unique and became nationally famous for a touchdown celebration dance—a high-kneed, running-in-place dance accentuated by spiking the ball. He was a good player, but I was still with the Chiefs after he left Kansas City. A lot of my teammates didn't care that he did his dance. I was always very careful—not that I was always successful—not to overcelebrate a touchdown or a big play. I didn't like to show up players on the other team. You can be joyful without overdoing it. I think Elmo overdid it with the dance, but it didn't bother me. I thought he was going to be a heck of a ballplayer, but he was never able to shake the injury bug. He never duplicated the success of his rookie season, 1971.

Ed Budde. Ed was a wild man, a guy who wouldn't take anything from anybody. He was a tremendous ballplayer—always fighting and always extremely aggressive.

One year Ed and Ernie Ladd got into it, really fighting, and Ernie had him bleeding from the mouth and nose. Ladd was a huge defensive lineman—an incredibly big man. And the "Big Cat," Ernie's nickname, was getting the better of Ed in the fight. But Ed never gave up and stayed at it. He didn't back off. Budde was the same way on the football field; he never gave up. He was the toughest son of a bitch I ever saw. My first couple of years with the Chiefs I was a little afraid of Ed—I don't really know why—but I learned a lot about what it takes to be a winner from him.

Ed didn't possess the most talent of our offensive linemen, yet in my opinion, he was still the best. He had a lot of heart and was a true, hard-nosed, never-let-anyone-whip-your-ass kind of guy.

Dave Hill. Another top lineman for the Chiefs in the 1960s and '70s was Dave Hill. Dave didn't have overwhelming talent, but he did have fantastic technique, great patience, and great knowledge of the game. I always thought he would have been a good line coach when his playing days were completed.

Dave was a big guy who weighed around 300 lbs., and that was big in the '60s and '70s. While he wasn't what I'd call a physical player, he made good use of his size and weight with perfect blocking techniques and fundamental knowledge of offensive line play.

Mo Moorman. Mo was hard and dangerous, a real I-don't-give-a-damn type of guy. He'd tear your ass up in a second. He was ferocious and unafraid. He may have been the best—at least talent-wise—offensive lineman I played with for the Chiefs.

Jim Tyrer. Jim had a head almost as big as mine, which is big. He was usually quiet and remained in the background. He hung out primarily with the guys on the offensive line. Jim was just Jim. But he was a great lineman—as good as Budde. Sadly, his life became another tragedy in the history of the Chiefs. Jim had a series of businesses fail following his retirement from the game. Despondent and giving up hope, he committed suicide in 1980.

E. J. Holub. First a linebacker and then the center on our 1969 championship team, E. J. was one of the team pranksters. He was infamous for depositing small and not-so-small dead animals in his teammates' beds at training camp. E. J. always had something going on—always playing a joke—whether it was in the clubhouse or somewhere else. He also did a lot of partying.

Jack Rudnay. Jack was the other center for the Chiefs during my playing days. He was a great guy, and I really enjoyed being around him. He gave me the nickname "T-Bag," and I never figured out where he got that—T-Bag. What Rudnay did for the ball club was tremendous. He kept everyone relaxed. On a scale of one to 10 in athletic ability, I'd put Rudnay at a five. But he was a 10 when it came to heart.

Fred Arbanas. Fred was one of the best I've seen at tight end, which is especially remarkable because he only had one good eye. He was amazing with his businesslike attitude. There was not much messing around from Fred. He always spoke his mind. I really admired him and how he overcame his handicap, not to just play professional football, but to be one of the best at his position. I also had great respect for the fact that he knew when to quit. Nobody told him to retire; he just knew when he couldn't play to the level he had been accustomed to. And Fred probably could've played another one or two years for sure.

Ed Podolak. Ed had a tremendous amount of belief in himself. He didn't have super athletic talent, but he was excellent at making things happen, and he was a great student of the game. He was a thinking football player. He wasn't a super back—not many guys are—

but he was a good teammate who gave 100 percent all of the time. Like some of the other jokers on the team, Ed was always dangerous at training camp. You had to watch him, because he would do almost anything.

Mike Garrett. Mike was a great football player, but I always thought Mike was a little strange for walking away from football the way he did. He let it be known he wanted to play baseball, and the Chiefs traded him in the middle of the 1970 season to San Diego. He had a shot with the Dodgers, but really didn't have the stuff of a major-league ballplayer by that time. He continued to play with the Chargers until 1973.

Garrett could run the ball, though, and could have easily been the team's feature back if given the opportunity. Mike never got close to anyone. He was a bit of a loner. He never got excited; I think I saw him get excited three times during his career. I know the guys on the offensive line liked to block for him because they knew he would get something when he ran. Mike should have been a guy who touched the ball 25 times a game, much like Priest Holmes did for the Chiefs in 2001 and 2002.

Robert Holmes. Bobby, "The Tank," was my man. He kept everybody on their toes and was always a lot fun and a lot of laughs. We also called him "Bob-O." We paired up on a 91-yard pass play in 1969 against the Dolphins, which was really just Bobby backing me up on a long pass play. I pulled a groin muscle at the end of my run and lateraled back to Bobby, who took the ball in for the score. He was from Southern, in the SWAC, and we did a lot of partying together when we were both with the Chiefs.

Mike Livingston. Mike was our second-string QB the last half of my career with the Chiefs. By today's standards, his size, strength and athletic ability would make him the starter for most teams in the NFL. He could throw the ball 80 yards—toss the ball into the upper deck. He was great when he filled in for Lenny during the 1969 season, and showed a lot of patience waiting for his turn to become the team's number-one quarterback. The Chiefs never gave him the respect he deserved, and were always talking about replacing him.

•••

My personal rule while playing was that I didn't really like any defensive players. They were the enemy, whether I was lining up against them in a game or they were wearing the same jersey I wore in practice. But I had some great ones as teammates in Kansas City, and it would be foolish of me to think we could have won any kind of championship without the Hall of Fame and Pro Bowl talent we had on our defense.

Willie Lanier. Willie and I had words once. I guess it was an argument. I grabbed him, but he threw me down. It was at that point I decided I better stay down and talk things over. As a person, I liked him. As a linebacker, he had no peer. His hits were so ferocious, so earth-shattering, he was lovingly called "Contact" by the rest of the Chiefs, but we also called him "Bear" or "Honeybear" because of his appearance. Willie was aggressive, robust and savvy, and he put some thunderous hits on our opponents. His speed, quickness, durability and size all contributed to his enormous success—and to the Chiefs' success—making him a true Hall of Famer.

Emmitt Thomas. I love Emmitt, but he beat on me constantly every day in practice. Along with Jim Marsalis, Emmitt should be in the Hall of Fame. He was one of the best in man-to-man coverage. For several years, there was nobody in the league better than Emmitt. I made him a better player and he did the same for me. If I had been a defensive back, I would have wanted to be like Emmitt. He coached the team as a player and has been an assistant coach in the NFL for many years with several different teams.

Jim Marsalis. He was every bit as good as Emmitt his first few years in the league, and, like Emmitt, he enjoyed beating on me during practice. He was the first cornerback ever taken in the first round of the draft by the Chiefs. Marsalis picked off just two passes his rookie season, which was a low number, because nobody threw at him. His presence in the Chiefs' secondary was so respected and he played so well that he was selected for the AFL All-Star Game as a rookie.

Buck Buchanan. Buck became the prototypical defensive lineman when he came to Kansas City as a first-round draft pick from Grambling. He was tough and had speed, agility and great body control. Buck was even tougher when you got on him about not being tough. He would get violently mad. He always played hard. He did it all— he stopped the run and rushed the passer. He could really destroy a team. He straightened me out several times and helped me a lot. I always returned the favors. Buck told me before he passed away in 1992 that he thought I was the best athlete he ever saw in his life. That was very touching, and I got choked up. To hear something like that from a man who was on his deathbed...I miss him a lot.

Buck Buchanan, my dear friend. (Photo provided by the Kansas Collection, U. of Kansas Archives)

Bobby Bell. Bobby was the only guy on the team who could have played almost any position. He was the first Chiefs player enshrined in the Pro Football Hall of Fame.

"Bobby Bell is the greatest outside linebacker who ever played the game," Coach Stram said of Bell at his Hall of Fame induction. "He is the only player I have seen who could play any position on a team and that team could still win."

"I didn't care where I played," Bell said. "All I cared about was winning."

Jim Lynch. The Chiefs' third great linebacker, Jim Lynch, never received his due because he played with Lanier and Bell. But I can tell you he was every bit as valuable as those other two guys were, especially when opposing teams thought they could run away from Bell. I really believe that the three of them, Bell, Lanier and Lynch, formed the greatest linebacker trio in the history of pro football.

Jan Stenerud. Jan never had enough to do in practice, so I tried to make him into a wide receiver. The other receivers and I would get him to run drills with us. And that gave us one extra break in the rotation of players running routes and patterns. When you run 10-, 20-, 30-yard routes, it can get tiresome. He couldn't catch very well—he got hit in the head a few times—but he tried and was actually a big help in a lot of our workouts.

"I try to catch it, Otis," he would cheerfully say in his Norwegian accent, "but I don't catch it very good." We had a lot of fun in those practices.

Of course, as a kicker, Jan meant everything to us.

As far as the 1971 Christmas game against Miami goes, I don't know how he made it afterward. He's still asked about that game, more than 30 years later. It took a lot of heart and a lot of guts to continue, and the fact that he's a Hall of Famer says volumes about what everyone else thought of him.

Jerrel Wilson. Jerrel was called "The Duck." Quack, quack, quack. He was an outdoorsman—he liked hunting and fishing—and I guess that's where the nickname came from. But man, could he kick the ball! He was just as valuable as any other weapon we had on the team, maybe more so. I think he should definitely be in the Hall of Fame. Just look at his numbers. He led the league in punting four times—an NFL record—averaged 43.6 yards per punt for his career, was named to three Pro Bowls, and played for 15 seasons. Hall of Fame numbers? You bet. The Duck was also our emergency QB, RB, FB and TE—just the all-around emergency player—and he was one hell of a punter.

•••

The 1972 season was a disaster. The Dolphins kicked our ass in the first-ever regular-season game at Arrowhead Stadium, 20-10. We didn't win a home game until we beat the Raiders in November, and we finished the year with just three wins at the new stadium. We had been undefeated at Municipal in 1971 and lost only three total games at home the previous four years. We even lost to the Eagles at home, and they were winless coming into the game. I don't know if it was the new stadium or that we just weren't very good. Personally, I caught 57 passes again, but accumulated almost 300 fewer yards. The Chiefs finished at 8-6, a record much better than our performance indicated, and the rumblings that the team was "too old" started.

Arrowhead Stadium was not conducive to our team or our fans when the facility first opened. The intimacy of the old stadium was gone forever, and we didn't respond well to the new atmosphere. And that artificial turf was killer. But regardless of the new stadium and other excuses, we weren't very good and our level of play dropped tremendously in just one season.

The next year, 1973, we made a bit of a rally. Kansas City's "old men" made a run for the division title late in the year, but a humiliating blowout loss to the Raiders in the divisional showdown at Oakland by a score of 37-7 ended our hopes of returning to postseason play. I caught just 34 passes and scored only four TDs in our anemic pass offense. The Chiefs' final 1973 record was 7-5-2.

The bottom dropped out of everything in 1974. We were lousy from start to finish, winning only fives games. The transition players Stram had added to the club in the previous two years still weren't as good as the older guys—me, Lanier, Bell, Emmitt, Lenny and Buck. Our defense wasn't bad, giving up 293 points, but we only scored 233 points. I had a very disappointing season, catching just 24 passes and scoring only two touchdowns. I also missed four games because of my knee. It was the Chiefs' first losing season since 1963, and somebody had to pay for the poor performance.

So Hank Stram was fired.

When they fired Hank, to me, it was as bad as when Al Gore lost the presidency. Although Hank and I had had our share of problems through the years, he was still the man, had always been the man. And I think he still respected me. I was sorry for Hank and his family. He had given so much to Kansas City, but in the end, there were too many people against him in the front office. It almost seemed like a payback situation because people started throwing daggers at him. It really wasn't a good thing. I have no idea what they might have been paying him back for; we always won before his final season. Hank didn't come back to Kansas City for three or four years, until he became the head coach for the New Orleans Saints, and then he beat the Chiefs.

There was a time of transition after he left—changes that affected me personally. Paul Wiggin was named as the Chiefs' new head coach, and his short tenure was not a good time for the organization or me. It's difficult when you're told how great you are for so many

It was a sad day for me when the Chiefs fired Hank Stram. (Photo courtesy of the Taylor Family Collection)

years, and I wanted to do things my way on the field. I guess Wiggin deserved the right to do them his way, but I didn't like it.

Who was Paul Wiggin? He came in and was going to save the franchise, but he didn't know what the hell he was doing. He wasn't great, and I wasn't the only one on the team who felt that way. He did not know what he was doing. He didn't hurt the team any, but he certainly didn't save it, either. Wiggin didn't extend me the respect I deserved; he didn't know what respect was all about. He thought of himself as a good player. But hiring him to coach in the NFL was a mistake. I had to speak to him as a player, but I did that as little as possible.

"The whole notion of the game kind of changed when the Chiefs started playing at Arrowhead Stadium. When we were in the old stadium, it was just like playing in a cotton field. At the new stadium, I think the whole concept of the game turned around. It became corporate. They wanted the VIP seats and suites. I think that's when they disturbed a lot of the fans. Everyone wanted tickets to the Wolf Pack and they wanted the same type of seats [in the new stadium] that they had at Municipal. They came up with some different rules. They had guys all over the stadium. They weren't thinking of the fans any more. They were just thinking of the nice stadium and all that stuff. They went to artificial turf, and I think that took away from the game. Artificial turf was not as comfortable as the dirt. Here we were, with the greatest grass man in the world—George Toma—and they put artificial turf in instead of regular grass. A lot of guys started getting rug burns and other nagging injuries. More people got hurt—bruised up. I liked the old stadium, the closeness of the fans right behind the bench. Arrowhead was not the same. It didn't have the same feeling. You go to the old stadium, you had a dogfight on your hands. It was kind of hard to beat us in that stadium. I know they needed mores seats and all that stuff, but I think we lost something there for a long time."

—Bobby Bell

•••

I was hanging out with a few of my friends in California during the off season in the early 1970s, not doing much of anything except enjoying the weather and the good times. You know…partying. A couple of things about California and Los Angeles: If you don't have enough money when you're there, it's like you don't have anything at all. The other thing is: If you're in California long enough, sooner or later you'll meet someone who knows a friend of a friend who works in the motion picture business. Ron Law was that friend, and he knew just about everyone in and around Hollywood. The opportunity arose for me to be an extra in a movie, and I took it. Lincoln Kilpatrick, an action/adventure actor who starred in primarily black movies, lined up the part for me. Rafer Johnson, the great Olympic decathlon champion, was also in the movie, which was titled *Soul Soldier*.

The storyline for the movie was pretty simple. Following the Civil War, a select cavalry unit made up of former slaves was stationed in Texas to patrol the Mexican border. I was one of the select soldiers in the unit, a "soul soldier." I got to wear one of the cool uniforms—I still love uniforms—and rode a horse, something I always enjoyed. I had one special line:

"Whoooa!"

This was the movie poster from Soul Soldier. *(Photo courtesy of the Taylor Family Collection)*

Never a major release, the movie came out in 1972, although the Houston area played up my appearance quite a bit. "Houston's Otis Taylor in *Soul Soldier*"—that kind of stuff was in the movie ads in the newspapers. I didn't make a dime on the movie, but somewhere there's the promise of money on a piece of paper.

"We went to see the movie Otis was in in Houston. A lot of people did, because they were so shocked he was in a movie. It was called Soul Soldier. *I'm sitting in the movie theater, and of course there were a lot of people in there that knew us, but also a lot who didn't know our family. I think Otis had one word to say. He was in a military get-up. Looking at the picture of him on the horse makes me*

The movie star—ha! That's me on the left, trying to remember how to ride a horse. (Photo courtesy of the Taylor Family Collection)

laugh and brings back the memories. In the movie, you could see him from a distance, and then all of a sudden they rode up to this log cabin where the officers would be and some of them had started getting off the horses. You could see him then, really well."

—Florence Odell Taylor

• • •

In 1972, I got a call from Joanne Beebe, a reading consultant for the Kansas City Public Schools. The schools, she told me, were desperate for reading material that would be appealing to intermediate children. Was there any way I could help her and the schools? A way to help kids touched my heart, and from our initial conversation, as well as the many that followed, *The Otis Taylor Book* was developed. It's one of my proudest contributions to the Kansas City area.

The book is a remedial reader about my life for eight- and nine-year-olds. The sections of the book included a statement to students and teachers, my handprint, my life story, Warpaint (the Chiefs' mascot), and other items set up to pique the kids' interest in reading. This is the opening statement to the teachers who used the book:

"Behind any person there has to be someone working. Someone who cares and makes things happen. So, my statement to kids, basically, would include a statement to teachers. Kids today are, I like to say, "up on things." They need to be treated as persons, as individuals. That's the way Hank Stram treats us—as individuals. No two of us are alike.

"I am doing this solely for boys and girls with the only remuneration being personal satisfaction in serving others."

It was really a pretty cool book, and I enjoyed helping put it together. But I didn't stop with just the book; I went to classrooms, met many, many children, and tried to stress what I felt was the number-one message in the book: "It's not where you come from. You have to have a will to do. And you have to form the will within yourself if there's no help from others.

"Apply yourself while you're in school. Stay out of trouble. And today that's hard to do!"

I didn't get paid for helping with the book, and I'm not sure I would have accepted the money if it was offered. The book itself turned out to be very successful, a big hit with the kids. If my information helped a few kids turn things around and helped them with their reading, I feel great about it. A funny note about the book: More than a year after it came out, several copies of the book started "disappearing" throughout the school district.

Looking and feeling cool with my sister Odell. (Photo courtesy of the Taylor Family Collection)

Kids were stealing *The Otis Taylor Book*. I have to admit, I was kind of proud.

•••

One of the things I really enjoyed was playing basketball in the off season. A group of about 10 Chiefs players got together and barnstormed all over the Midwest, playing high school faculty teams, amateur teams, corporate teams and small-town teams. If someone had a team and wanted to play the Kansas City Chiefs, we were there. A lot of people thought we were just going out there to play—to have fun. Wrong. It was serious business, and it didn't matter who we were playing, we'd beat 'em to death physically if we could.

"The one real scare we had flying on a small plane to a basketball game, I can't remember a whole lot about it; just that it was very, very quiet in the plane. Nobody said anything. We were having a tough time landing at the downtown airport because the wind was so strong. The guy made about three or four passes trying to land and each time couldn't do it. Finally, he said, 'We're going down this time—one way or the other.' He caught it on the ground. Everybody got right off the plane, got in their cars and went home. Nobody said a thing. A funny thing...we used to go on some of these basketball trips and take three little planes that only held about four people each. We were going down to the Lake of the Ozarks to play one afternoon and one of the pilots couldn't make it for some reason or other. Mike Sensibaugh, a defensive back on the Chiefs, had been taking flying lessons, and he said, 'I can fly the plane. Who wants to go with me?' So me and Otis got in the plane with him. We flew down there and everything was fine. Otis told him before we started, 'I don't want any funny business.' Mike was a real prankster sort of guy. So we flew down there, found the airport and were going to land and Mike couldn't help himself. He had to do a couple of loop-de-loops and dive down at a farmhouse and stuff. I mean, Otis went crazy. He said, 'I'm going to kill you if we ever get out of this plane.' We played down in Texas, Oklahoma, Kansas, Nebraska, Iowa, Missouri, Illinois, Arkansas. We even did a stint one time with Marcus Haynes, the great Harlem Globetrotters player, who left the Trotters and formed his own team. We were the stooges for his team to play for about 10 or 15 games. That was a pretty good gig there. We had a lot of fun."

—Mike Livingston

•••

"What made Otis stand out is that when we were in practice, or whatever we were doing, he wanted to win. Those basketball games, I guarantee you, he wasn't out there jacking around. He was a winner. And the guy who was playing against him, Otis wanted to humiliate him. He had a killer instinct."

—Dave Hill, Chiefs Offensive Tackle, 1963-74

I was pretty good on the basketball court. I couldn't shoot worth a damn, because we never did practice. I could jump and dribble and dunk pretty good. And I could do all the other things that were needed to be a basketball player. Buck, Dave Hill, Emmitt Thomas, Ed Budde, Mike Livingston, Jim Kearney, Bobby Bell, Willie Lanier, and few of the other players on the football team rotated on and off the squad. Hill was pretty good, and of course Bell could play because he was such a great all-around athlete. Ed would come in for layups, and he really got in the other guy's face. For a bunch of football players on the court, we were pretty good. We did lose a few, but we thought we were the Philadelphia '76ers. The stands were always packed whenever and wherever we played, and sometimes we played three or four games a week. We made a lot of money, too, which was important.

Some of those guys we played against really worked hard. They all wanted to say they beat the Chiefs. Sometimes we played the faculty of a school or a couple of the businessmen around town who had played high school ball 30 or 40 years before. We'd beat the crap out of those teams. Sometimes we had to work to stay in the game, and, as I stated earlier, we lost some. We usually played every off season, but quit when the injuries stared to pile up. Actually, we were advised that we should stop playing.

"I warmed the bench when we played basketball. We had some pretty good basketball players, Otis and Bobby Bell, David Hill, Jerrel Wil-

The Chiefs' basketball team, front row, from left: Emmitt Thomas, Jerrel Wilson, me, and Mike Livingston; back row, from left: Ed Budde, Dave Hill, Buck Buchannan, and Bobby Bell. (Photo courtesy of Ed Budde)

son, and Mike Livingston. Jerrel and I and would just give relief to the athletes. We warmed the bench in that particular sport. Otis was a heck of a basketball player. So were Bobby and David Hill. David Hill could really shoot. And Emmitt Thomas played, too. We had a pretty good basketball team. We used to have pickup games once, twice a week for about three months. We had a lot of fun, and we even traveled to San Antonio once."

—Ed Budde

•••

"We had so many close calls on those little old Cessna planes. We'd leave from Grain Valley and we'd have a headwind of maybe 25-30 knots. We weren't moving at all. Going out to western Kansas, we got lost in the fog and clouds and lost our communication. We ended up in Lincoln, Nebraska. We followed the railroad tracks, the plane got down so low. We had to watch out for Dave Hill, who was in the plane with the pilot, and that was scary. I was cool, sitting there saying my prayers. One time in western Kansas, the landing gear wouldn't come down. I think that was with Dave Hill, myself and the pilot. On the Cessna they have a little crank in the back so that if the gear doesn't go down electrically, you can kind of wind it down. And we flew around and around the airport for more than 10 minutes until it finally kicked down."

—Jim Kearney

•••

"I pulled my old high school team together and we beat the Chiefs' basketball team. They never lived that down. I was a rookie then and they were making money, playing basketball in the off season, and they all came up to Atlantic, Iowa, my hometown. I put my old high school team together and we had had some great athletes—went to the state tournament two years in a row. We pummeled them. And that includes Bobby Bell, Livingston, Emmitt Thomas, Otis and David Hill. After the game we all went to my mom and daddy's house and ate chili. They had to drive a gravel road to get there because they were repairing Highway 71. When Livingston, Otis and everybody got there they went, "Goddang, Podolak, we heard you were from the sticks, but we've been on a gravel road for 30 minutes!" They made a hundred bucks a game as I remember it,

which was a lot of money then. Bobby Yarborough, the Chiefs' equipment manager organized the games for them."

—Ed Podolak

•••

I owned a nightclub in Kansas City for a while—The Flanker—over at 59th and Prospect. I originally talked to Ollie Gates of Gates Bar-B-Q about opening and owning a club, and he helped me set things up. The one thing I didn't do or realize was that I wasn't prepared to own and operate a nightclub—it took a lot of money. I invested a lot, and I trusted a couple of guys who stole from me. I think for every dollar I put into that club, they stole two. It finally got to the point where my money ran out, and I found out about the stealing.

Too bad, because it was one of the most outstanding clubs in Kansas City. It was beautiful inside—the decorations were pretty classy. Everybody knew about The Flanker. Unfortunately, I didn't have the know-how or the time to manage it right. I needed to be there all the time, and I couldn't, especially during the football season. It was open for two years, and if the stealing wasn't bad enough, when it ran out and we closed, Uncle Sam came after me and hammered me on taxes. I guess I wasn't responsible enough at that point in my life.

It was hard to accept The Flanker closing, but Mr. Gates told me if you own something, you have to be there. Nobody works for free, and they are going to give you one and take two if they see the opportunity. People still remember The Flanker today as a nice club, and I know a lot of people—sophisticated people—enjoyed it there.

•••

I once said I'd eat dog food if the price was right.

I was angry for a long time about the total absence of black players doing product endorsements, not just in Kansas City, but across the country. I was eager to do them, and I know I would have helped any product I endorsed. Otis Taylor was a well-known name in the early 1970s. I wanted to use my name and make a little cash.

Nobody wanted me.

Everybody will pat you on the back and tell you how great you are, but they won't give you an endorsement opportunity to talk about their product. Why? I don't mean anything personal, but if Bill Grigsby can do all the commercials he does and be successful, then I know I could have done it, too. I have to praise Mr. Gates for giving me the few endorsements I have had, telling the world how great Gates Bar-B-Q is. I enjoyed doing them; it was something new, but I knew I would get better and better as I kept doing them. There is only so much you can do for one product. Honestly, if someone had come up with a dog food commercial, I'd have done it. But I was never asked, and it has to be because I am black. There is no other reason.

Lenny has done endorsements for years and is very good at it. And there were guys who played after we did who got to do commercials. The young kids

Here I am helping Ollie Gates and his son with the advertising and distribution of his wonderful sauce in the early 1970s. (Photo provided by the Kansas City Chiefs)

today have it much better, and many of today's Chiefs, black and white alike, do commercials. But I still feel cheated on the limited opportunities offered to me by the businesses in Kansas City and at the national level, too.

•••

My last game with the Chiefs was the first game of the 1975 season against the Broncos in Denver, which we lost, 37-33. I didn't catch a pass. My ailing left knee finally got the better of me, and after fighting constant fluid and putting up with the pain of draining it all the time, I was put on the injured reserve list—I was out for the year.

On June 1, 1976, the Chiefs traded me to the Houston Oilers. Kansas City was my full-time home, and I intended to stay there after my playing days ended. But finishing my career in my hometown wasn't a bad idea. Mom and Dad were there, and I'd be away from Paul Wiggin. I had talked to Houston's coach, Bum Phillips, and was looking forward to the new challenge.

My football time in Kansas City was over, and it was going to be a thrill to play for the Oilers one last year in my hometown.

But it never happened.

A lot people don't remember because the trade happened so quickly. If I was going anywhere, I said I wanted to go to Houston because that was home. It was scary, though, because I really didn't want to go. They wanted just one season in Houston. I gave it all I could, but my knee just wouldn't let me play. It was shot, and my time in Houston ended before it began. There was no final hurrah, no last go 'round. The choices before me were limited and I had to do something I didn't want to do. After all the games, catches and touchdowns, I finally made a move that wasn't awe-inspiring or impossible to imagine.

I retired from professional football.

12

THE TALENT SCOUT

I had been out of football for three years, and the money I had saved from deferred payments on my last contract with the Chiefs was almost gone. I wanted a job in football, wanted to stay in Kansas City, and more than anything else, I wanted to be a part of the Chiefs' organization.

Those weren't going to be easy objectives to accomplish.

The Chiefs have never been an organization that hired former players as coaches, and only a couple of guys have been hired for jobs in the front office. It's a policy that, I guess, came from Lamar Hunt himself and is one that I've never understood. In contrast, the Raiders have hired several former players, from Art Shell as head coach to other positions right down the line of their entire organization. They take care of their former players—treat them like family—and they're not the only team in the NFL that does so. Still, I was determined to work for the Chiefs—the organization that had always been like a second family to me, at least when Coach Stram was around.

I found out a scouting position was available with the Chiefs, and I wanted it. I knew football, I knew football players, and I had always been a pretty good judge of the talent level of my teammates. I made it known that I wanted the position.

I met with the Chiefs' general manager, Jim Schaff, president Jack Steadman, and Les Miller, the oldest scout on the staff at that time. Outwardly they were open to me joining the scouting staff, but I never got the feel from them that they really wanted me. It was on a Thursday that the four of us met in Steadman's office, and they started talking about how hard it was on the road and how hard it would be to scout, that it's a lonesome life and a somewhat tedious job. And then they offered me a contract with an absolutely ridiculous salary—less than $20,000 a year. I don't believe that they wanted to give me the job, and the paltry salary they offered was intended to scare me away. I think it was Steadman who said, "Why don't you wait until Monday to let us know if you decide to take it or not?"

Something hit me right then—clicked in my brain—that told me not to wait.

"No," I said, "I'll take it now. And I'll be to work tomorrow."

I think that shocked them because the salary they offered was insulting. But I took it anyway and reported to work the next day as the newest member of the Kansas City Chiefs' scout team. I can say now that they understated the hardships of being a scout, and it turned out to be a lot harder than anything I had ever undertaken in my life.

"When Otis got out of football, he had a hard time because he didn't have a job. I remember an article in the paper after he retired titled, 'Where Are the Cheers Now?' It went something like, 'Remember when everybody was cheering him and he was the greatest, and then when he got out of football, it seemed like they just threw him away like a piece of meat.' So when that article came out, I think the Chiefs gave him a job as a scout. I'd go out to training camp at William Jewel College, and Otis was out there coaching the receivers. I talked to Otis about it. Why didn't they hire him as a coach? He's

The Chiefs' scouting team in 1980, front row, from left: Les Miller, Tommy O'Boyle, and J. D. Helm; back row: Bobby Gill and me. (Photo courtesy of the Taylor Family Collection)

got the balance. He'd been through the mills before. He knew the operation of the NFL. He knew the defensive back thing. Instead they gave him a job as a scout, and he was pretty disappointed."

—Jim Kearney

An NFL scout leads a lonesome life. The constant travel can really bog you down. But as I began working for the Chiefs, I found out that on top of the lonely life, I'd also have to endure working with people who didn't—or refused to—get along with me. Basically, there were a lot of rednecks then in the Chiefs' scouting department. But Tommy O'Boyle, one of the Chiefs' veteran scouts, was a good man, and he told me he'd be in my corner and help me as much as he could.

I've always had a thing for nice clothes; I always like to look sharp. So naturally I'd wear good-looking clothes to work—really cool suits that were pretty expensive, along with alligator shoes. And the guys at work, the other scouts, would throw out little jokes about what I was wearing. I tried to explain that when I bought a $300-$400 suit—expensive in those days—that it was just like the trucks I saw outside with four guns in the back window. They loved guns; I loved clothes. I used to ask them, "What's so different? You like to get out of the truck and walk the fields shooting rabbits and birds." I don't like to hunt and I'm scared of guns anyway. I've always been able get along with anybody—that's always been one of my strengths—but I hate it when people nibble at me, trying to be funny, or just being downright nasty.

Here's a good example of the kind of stuff I had to endure. One of our scouts was reading a scouting report on a top prospect in a meeting. "Okay, his name is Joe Blow, he's six feet six, 279 pounds, runs a 4.78 40-yard dash." Then he read a few more details about the guy and finished with "and he's married to a white girl." That hit me the wrong way, because I took it for exactly what it was—racial bullshit. I was the next one to talk about a prospect, and after I finished with the details on the kid, I said, "and he's not married to a white girl."

My boss called me into his office later and I had to apologize for my comment. Things like that went on. Scouting, even within our own department, was a cutthroat thing. But Tommy was the one guy on the scouting staff who really took the time to teach me what I needed to know—what to look for when I went to a school, make sure I was always on time, and above all else, stay and be sharp—and get me started in scouting.

The routine I went through scouting college prospects didn't change very much during my 11 years on the staff. At first we flew everywhere, but after fighting airline scheduling problems too many times, we started renting cars. I might drive all the way to North Dakota, do my scouting in that area—I hardly ever stayed out more than 12 days—and then I'd leave my car at the airport and fly home. I'd bring my suitcase full of dirty clothes, wash them, go into the office and turn in my reports, get another schedule, fly back to pick up my car, and drive to the next location. I worked that routine until I'd visited the 30-plus schools that I was assigned.

On my very first trip as a scout, I went to Nebraska, and I was so amazed. I hung out with some of the other scouts who were there, getting drinks and talking. There were RVs all over the place—and not just the little ones—the huge plug-in models. I asked some of the other guys where the RVs came from, and one guy said the belonged to the farmers. They parked their tractors on Saturday morning, hopped into their RV and drove to Lincoln to see the Huskers.

Nebraska never treated the scouts very well. It didn't matter who you were; you sat in the stands. It was the same thing with Michigan and Michigan State. I climbed so many steps at Michigan, and there were always little old ladies or old men on crutches going up those steps, too.

If I was in the press box, I was able to scout with a little pizzazz. But in the stands, people were always jumping up and down, and that made it hard to find and focus on a specific player on the field. I scouted Neil Smith, who became a great Pro Bowl defensive lineman for the Chiefs that year. He was something else.

The main thing to remember about scouting talent is this: It still boils down to a simple thing that I think a lot of people don't understand and don't really want to understand—it's still blocking, tackling, and running. Whatever else they want to make out of it, it's still those three fundamental aspects.

One of my grandest visits was to the University of Oklahoma. I got to meet Barry Switzer, the Sooners' coach. I really like that man. He was one of the nicest guys and was always around when I was there looking at his players. A lot of coaches thought scouts interrupted their kids' study time, or were a disruption to practice, but not Barry. He talked to me at length and always had good stories. Once he told me about a recruiting trip he made to Houston, and how the beans, rice and chicken he ate at the kid's house were the best he ever had. Little, simple stories like that. Barry was a hell of a guy and always made sure I had enough film—we watched film of prospects playing constantly. He made my trips to Oklahoma more than worthwhile, and I looked forward to going there.

I went to Michigan State and had a great time because that's where Ed Budde, my old teammate, went to school. I went up there to see Kirk Gibson, a receiver for the Spartans. He thrilled me. I could hear the excitement in my own voice when I talked to him. Gibson could have given the NFL some hell if he had stayed with football—he opted for baseball and became a star outfielder for the Tigers and Dodgers. He ran a 4.35, was 220 pounds, and could really catch the ball. When I scouted him, the quarterback came out and threw him some balls. He kept doing what I asked him to do and then wanted to do more. It was something to watch a guy of his quality. I really wish he would've stayed with football, because he was a great wide receiver for Michigan State.

I looked at other receivers like Jerry Rice—I knew he was going to be spectacular and pushed very hard for the Chiefs to draft him—and Sterling Sharpe, who also had a quality career before he got hurt. Hell, a blind man could have seen Jerry Rice and known that he was going help any football team—that he was going to be great. I was also impressed with Don Beebe, who turned out to be a very good receiver for the Bills and Packers.

> *"It really wasn't that bad, at least for me, when Otis traveled all the time as a scout. We had our son, but my mother was living with us at the time and she was a big help with the house stuff—errands and other things. The biggest adjustment was getting used to Otis being gone so long; sometimes he would be on the road for more than two weeks. It was harder on him than me, because that's a long time to be gone, carrying bags from one little town to the next. It was hard on our son, too. He would just get used to his dad being home and then Otis would have to leave again—they were and are really close."*
>
> —Regina Hill Taylor, Otis's wife

At the end of a road trip—let's say I got home on a Thursday—I hugged my wife, played with my baby and then on Monday morning went back out. I spent so many depressing hours on the road that there was many a time when I would drive down the highway with tears in my eyes. I thought about where I was going and about where I was headed in life. I was smoking and drinking more and more. I used to listen to Marvin Gaye, and sometimes I would pull up to a light and he'd be singing one of those love songs, and after being on the road for almost two weeks, the tears would start coming out of my eyes. Once I stopped next to a lady who looked over at me and asked, "Are you all right?" It was a tough life out there.

A lot of the other scouts were pretty helpful to me, giving me information and clues. The scouting profession had couple of a little cliques, and if you were in the clique, your job was much easier. One guy would take all heights, weights, and speeds; five other guys would test the players. Sharing information really cut down the amount of time each of us had to spend on a particular kid.

The Chiefs bought into two different scouting combines. A combine supplied the same material to about 12 different teams. Early material was written up on a kid when he was a junior, letting the teams know who was worthy of being put on their list to be looked at the following year. They invited hundreds of guys to the combine in Indianapolis, and they have the kids do every kind of exercise there is: lateral movements, leaping, running the 40, an obstacle course, and lifting weights. It's very hard. Teams get together to cut down on expenses because scouting can be very costly. The more specialized information comes from the scouting trips—one scout might not see what someone else sees in a player. That's why some players drafted in the eighth and ninth round make the team and why some guys who don't get drafted at all can make a team, too. A lot of the scouts in the NFL are buddy-buddy and they just hand off the information they gather to each other. The group that I worked with in Kansas City wasn't bad, but it wasn't good either, because I know I was disliked for being a former player.

We scouted as a group, and that was the standard procedure. The whole group was responsible, wrong or right, for whomever the Chiefs drafted. So while I might have done a lot of the final ratings breakdowns on the wide receivers each year, my scouting reports covered every good player at the schools I traveled to. My reports on quarterbacks, running backs and linemen helped us determine the overall order for those positions as well. The pre-draft meetings were held in Kansas City, and everybody put in long hours of preparation. For the final two weeks before any of the drafts I participated in, we worked until at least midnight or one every day.

Our system for scoring and grading a player was pretty simple. We graded each guy on a scale from 1.0 to 10.0. When you rated a guy at 7.0, he was going to make the team. And if he was rated higher than that, he was a sure bet to be a first-year starter. If I gave a kid a 4.5, he was way down on the list and might be able to make the club as a free agent. We'd take all the information we gathered—from our scouting reports, the combines and coaches—and sort it out. For example, some things a receiver has to have are good hands and speed. He doesn't have to have exceptional speed, because I've seen some guys who run a 4.5 or 4.6 and make it just as often as the faster guys.

At the end of the season, I'd get 12 receivers to double check, and one of the other Chiefs scouts would get, say, 12 offensive linemen, and then we'd go out and make another report on them. I'd rate all those wide receivers and name the ones who were the top guys. When I thought a player was exceptional I stuck my neck out for him, and I would do that without any doubt in my mind.

> *"I'm not knocking the Chiefs down, but they've never hired from within—not one guy from their Super Bowl teams. Other teams do. You look around the league and Joe Green went to Pittsburgh to coach, he was a great player. Everybody can't be a coach, but Otis was qualified to coach. Dave Hill was qualified, too. Lenny [Dawson] could have, if he chose to, because he knew the game."*
>
> —Jim Kearney

When John Mackovic was hired as the Chiefs' head coach in 1983, it was with the stipulation that he would select our first-round pick in the draft. That was the year of the great quarterback class in college football—Elway, Marino, Kelley, etc.—but Todd Blackledge was the guy Mackovic wanted. We didn't have time to get upset, because they basically already had him signed to a contract. The worst thing about Mackovic's selection—and Blackledge didn't pan out at all as a starting quarterback—was that we could have had Dan Marino.

There's a funny thing among the scouting ranks in the NFL—rumors spread faster than a deadly cancer—and Marino was victimized in the rumor mill. Marino liked to party and he liked women—

a real fast and loose guy. So what, right? But some ugly stories started circulating about drug use and alcohol problems and Marino's pre-draft stock dropped tremendously. On the flip side, Blackledge was the model student, athlete and son—the all-American boy-next-door type. So Blackledge was the guy.

The Chiefs weren't the only team who passed on Marino. He dropped all the way to the bottom of the first round and the Dolphins snatched him up. Blackledge played in Kansas City for five years, but he never came close to reaching the expectations the Chiefs had for him. He ended up being a damn good football announcer, whereas Marino broke almost every passing mark in the NFL record book.

The last few years of my scouting career, they started asking very personal questions about the prospects. They wanted to know what the kid's daddy was doing or if the mama was divorced. They wanted to know about character. They wanted to know any little thing that might keep them from getting their money's worth out of a draft pick. I looked for little clues about the guys I was scouting everywhere. I'd go to a school, see an assistant coach, and try to buddy up; maybe he'd talk to me a little more because he was interested in getting a job and getting out of wherever he was. I might have had five different players on my list and I needed to know about their characters. Is he a troublemaker? How does he practice? I got as much as I could, and I'd say I got the information from a coach and put his name in the report, too. Maybe one of the players we were looking at was a complete asshole, or his daddy could have been an addict. He might have had two brothers who played football, but never got through college and quit playing.

There were written standardized tests, and most of the players didn't want to take a test. Sometimes I found a trainer and they often gave me a lot of good information; but you have to judge whether it's good stuff or not. That's how I got my information, almost like a detective.

I did a lot more for the Chiefs than just scouting. Carlos Carson, a wide receiver with the Chiefs from 1980-89, came to me in the scouting room one day early in his career. He asked, "Mr. Taylor, can I talk to you awhile?"

I said sure.

"They won't throw me the ball," he said. "So I want to get away from here. What do you think?"

"Carlos, do you want me to tell you a lie or do you want the truth?" I asked him. "It's just like this: you aren't doing a goddamn thing. You're not catching the ball. You have to make it so they have no choice but to throw to you. Catch 50 balls before practice. Catch 50 after practice. You're not doing a thing and he has no reason to throw it to you. The quarterback will not throw you the ball if you can't do anything."

The next year Carlos had a record number of catches and made All-Pro.

I would tell a kid, just like I've told my son Otis, to do the same thing. I don't believe in the soft talk. I believe that if a guy comes and asks for advice, tell him the truth. I told Carlos the truth, and then I worked with him. Some guys asked me to watch them and see what they were doing wrong, and I'd tell them.

Almost every year while I was a scout, I helped with the coaching of the wide receivers at the Chiefs' training camp in Liberty, Missouri. For the most part, I think the receivers responded to my instructions and tried to do the things I taught them about receiving. I worked them hard: catching balls, steps, drills, cuts, and passes. The only mistake I made—and I probably would have had a better shot at coaching if I would have done this—was not going to some of the coaches' meetings during camp. The problem was that I couldn't go to a lot of meetings because as a scout I was evaluating the players for the cuts. The scouts were also the guys who told a player he was cut, and I never did like doing that. We'd have to go get the guy, and he would know exactly what was going on. A lot of the players would start crying. Some them deserved to be cut, but no matter, that is one of the toughest things to do—telling a guy he's gone.

Following the 1986 season, the Chiefs fired head coach John Mackovic and replaced him with Frank Gansz. Mackovic had taken the Chiefs back to the playoffs for the first time since we had lost to the Dolphins on Christmas Day back in 1971, and his reward was the chance to find another job. Mackovic, at least to me, was just becoming a good coach. If you watched him on the sidelines during games, he didn't really know what to do after something happened, good or bad. He didn't know how to react—whether to touch the guy, talk to him soft or hard. But his last season, he was starting to give the guys gestures and signs when they made a good play. Or he would come in for a minute and talk to a player about some way he messed up. He was aggressive with his feelings, and that was his only real fault the first three years in Kansas City. He's been a fine coach since, and not bad on television, either. And Frank Gansz? He didn't last more than two years, and even that was too long.

The National Football League Players Association (NFLPA) called a strike on Tuesday, September 22, 1987. The following week's games were canceled, but the owners decided to use replacement players and resume playing games on October 4. My job in that mess was to find players for the replacement team—not an easy task. I was talking with a player the Chiefs had cut in training camp about playing for us in the replacement games.

The striking players were on top of the hill outside the stadium, but before long, they came down to the One Arrowhead Drive entrance. The replacement player left the offices, but returned shortly, telling me the strikers had slashed his tires. We called AAA to see how much it would cost to replace the tires, and I went out with the kid to look at the car.

As I attempted to walk through the picket line, Jack Del Rio, one of the Chiefs' linebackers (current head coach of the Jacksonville Jaguars and a good guy) didn't recognize me. I guess he thought I was a replacement player, too. Del Rio started yelling "dirty scab" and "lowlife" at me, and then I yelled back. I may have been as much of an instigator as he was, because I was taking a firm line, too. I wasn't going to let anybody push me or run over me, and that's what Del Rio was trying to do. We yelled at each other and he rushed me. Remember, I was close to 50 years old at the time, and he was a strapping young linebacker. He grabbed me in a headlock and flipped me. I lost my balance as he tried to body-slam me, and I fell onto the gravel.

We wrestled around a little before Dino Hackett, another Chiefs linebacker who was toting a shotgun at the picket line, and someone else broke it up. Del Rio finally realized who I was and that I worked for the club. He said, "Hey, Otis, I used to love watching you. You were a great player." But he didn't know my affiliation with the team.

I have never really gotten over that, because I worked for the organization and did all I could to put a team back on the field and get some players to play during that strike. Nobody in the Chiefs organization offered any kind of satisfaction to me for going out and trying to be a good worker. After all was said and done, I was basically on my own. They didn't even give me any kind of recognition after getting my ass kicked.

I knew most of the players who were striking, and I had a lot of respect for them. And I had a lot of respect for what they were doing. But I had a job to do and they needed to give me the same respect. You had Nick Lowery, Bill Maas and all those other players out there. If I didn't feel like I could handle the situation or if they wanted to let me know what was going to happen, then that fight could have easily been avoided.

The thing that really hurt me most of all was that my sister called me later the same day. I tried to dress up a little bit that day and I had on a pair of loafers, but no socks, a common fashion thing at the time. I didn't think she'd seen the altercation even though the damn thing was on national television. I didn't want her to see it because our mother was sick and I didn't want either one of them to be upset. Odell saw it anyway, and she called to ask if mother could send me money for some socks. In the scuffle on the ground, my slacks were pulled up and when she saw my bare legs, she thought I couldn't afford any socks. Mother got on the phone. "I'll put the money in the mail today," she said. I told her, no, I had some socks.

No charges were filed against Del Rio, but I sued him, Chiefs player representative Nick Lowery, and the NFL Players Association for $1 million. The case was finally settled out of court two years later, but all I really wanted, in terms of personal satisfaction, was to have the Chiefs back me up. It was an ugly chapter in my time with the Chiefs.

Shortly after Carl Peterson took over as the Chiefs president and general manager, I went to work like I always did, ready to analyze prospects and do my other regular duties. Marty Schottenheimer was the new head coach, and I had hopes of becoming a member of the coaching staff. What happened next was something that I was completely and totally unprepared for.

They called me into the office and fired me—they fired a lot of us that day.

I might be wrong, but I think they sacked everybody who had a Super Bowl ring. It was a coup. In shock, I left and went home. One thing I'll never understand is how people can fire you but turn around and say how great a job you did. To that I say, "If I did such a good job, why am I walking out of here with a box in my hand?"

The loneliest feeling I've ever had in my life was the day I left that stadium and was no longer working for the Kansas City Chiefs. And there is one thing that I want to express maybe more than anything else I've written in this book: The worst situation that man, woman or beast has to go through is getting fired when everybody is telling you what a great job you did, as you walk out the door. There's nothing as sad as that. I could be a counselor on how it feels when you get fired. That was the worst feeling I've ever had in my life. I was fired from pro football, but I can relate to getting fired, period. It's a tough pill to swallow. Getting fired was like getting cut from the team. When I was a rookie at training camp, every day at 1:30 you'd hear a knock on someone's door. "Coach Stram wants to see you over in his office, and bring your playbook." I've seen some long faces that I should have taken a picture of as they were walking over to the administrative building where Hank's office was.

After the firing, my feelings for the Chiefs went from love-love-love to hate-hate-love-hate.

I never did get any support about being on the coaching staff. Shottenheimer told the biggest lie of the century. I worked hard in summer camp with the receivers and helped them become a force. But every time I turned around, they were telling me I didn't have enough experience. I thought I had enough skills from working with the wide receiver coaches during the course of my 10 years of scouting and working the summer camps. Somebody must have been thinking something else. Every time I asked for an interview or to just talk about it, I'd hear, "You better do what you gotta do and stop worrying about coaching." That was always my dream after I quit playing—to coach—and it never did come true.

13

A PEOPLE PERSON

Getting fired from my "family" wasn't an easy thing to recover from. I had always imagined that I'd be a part of the Chiefs organization for as long as I wanted. Instead, I was left in the position of not having the slightest idea of what my future held. I went to an employment agency, not just to find a job, but to also get a bearing on what kind of work I was best suited for outside of sports. The agency gave me tests and compiled profiles of my personality, skills, etc. When everything was pulled together, I knew what I was, what I had always been—a people person.

Someone who gets along with all races, genders, ages, etc.—that's a people person, and that's me. After that personal revelation, I found the perfect job at Blue Cross Blue Shield as a community ambassador. I owe a great deal to John Walker, the man at BCBS who hired and believed in me. I traveled to small towns all around the Kansas City area representing the company for various functions and gatherings sponsored by Blue Cross. Invariably, anywhere from 200 to 500 people would show up for the events, sometimes more. Through the years, I received many, many letters from people telling me how

My co-workers at Blue Cross Blue Shield, from left, Frank White, Jan Johnson, me and Alice Ellison. (Photo courtesy of the Taylor Family Collection)

pleased they were that I was with Blue Cross and that they felt my contributions were good.

I had the pleasure of working for and with two extraordinary women on a full-time basis in the last part of my tenure at BCBS—Alice Ellison and Jan Johnson. I always called Ms. Ellison the boss lady, but I called her that because she's just a great person and lady. I really depended on her and Jan. They're part of my family—my working family. Frank White, the Kansas City Royals' all-time great second baseman, was also a part of the community relations team.

Every year in August, Blue Cross and Blue Shield of Kansas City (and The Morgan Family Foundation in 2003), sponsors the Otis Taylor Celebrity Golf Tournament. All the local celebrities—

athletes and otherwise—play. It's a great honor for me and benefits the National Council on Alcoholism and Drug Dependence (NCADD) of Greater KC. The 10th annual tournament was held in 2003.

My time at Blue Cross and Blue Shield was special. I officially retired in 2002, but I still work with the company on a regular basis, attending events and helping when needed. I was at BCBS for 12 great, fulfilling years. I tried my best to live up to the company's expectations and high standards.

In addition to my work at BCBS, I have given my time and efforts to many different organizations in the Kansas City area. I've always been an active member in the Third & Long Foundation, the reading program started by the late Chiefs great Derrick Thomas. I've helped the Greater Kansas City Foundation, the Heritage Foundation, and the Rainbow Center. Numerous organizations around the city use my name for various activities—anything to help improve the city and make it better than ever.

•••

I first got married to a woman from Prairie View after I'd been with the Chiefs for a few years, but I was not ready to take on the full responsibility of marriage and it didn't last. But I feel I was blessed years later when I had the chance to marry again. I had been single for 13 or 14 years when I met Regina, and we really hit it off. Our son, Otis Taylor III, was born on August 31, 1985. Regina named him, not after me, but after my father—so she told me. Otis has been the joy of my life.

We waited, although I'm not sure why, to make sure it was the right thing to do and were married two years later. Otis was best man, and I never will forget that day...it was something else. I always tell people, I got my second chance, and I was Regina's first chance.

A happy day—Regina, Otis and me on our wedding day. (Photo courtesy of the Taylor Family Collection)

I'm Otis Taylor Jr., named after my dad. I know that sometimes things didn't go right for him, but the last 10 years of his life were probably the best between the two of us. It was the funniest thing to my dad when he would get on my wife's back and tease her all the time. He really had fun with that. She used to love talking to my dad because he inspired her. About two months before Otis was born he passed away, but in the five or six months before that he always acted like he knew Otis. We'd go down to Houston when Regina was pregnant, and it just tickled him to death. He told her that she looked so funny, and he would feel her tummy and say, "Jumpidy, jumpidy."

When Otis was born, I went into the room and saw my son for the first time. I couldn't believe it—I had a son!

"What are you going to name him?" I asked.

"Otis Taylor," Regina said.

"You don't have to name him after me. You can name him anything you like."

"I'm not naming him after you," she said.

"What are you talking about?"

"I'm naming him after your daddy. Your daddy is the headmaster. He's Otis Taylor Sr. This is Otis Taylor III. He's named after your daddy."

I said okay, fine with me. Regina had so much respect for Dad, and she wanted to honor him. I think that they had a bond that was not seen by anyone else because it was so personal. I'm glad he had a special relationship with her.

The real situation concerning my dad and me was that I had a hard time looking at things the way they were. I went to a psychologist because I had some problems believing and accepting that my dad was an alcoholic. I didn't want to hear it. It wasn't until his last five or 10 years that I really started to have a good relationship with him, and I've always been glad Regina named our son after him.

Otis has been the wonder of my life, and no man could have asked for a better son. He earned a football scholarship to Missouri Southern, where he'll play defensive back or wide receiver. Otis was also a very good basketball player at Raytown High. But it's not just the athletic accomplishments I'm proud of. He's a fine young man, in all aspects, and I know he'll do well in school beyond what he does on the football field. Watching him grow, learn and play sports was very, very special. No man could love his son more.

"One of the really impressive things about my relationship with my father is that it doesn't matter how many arguments we get into or

how many disagreements we have, I always know that he cares about me. He always brags on me to everyone. He's so proud of me and loves me so much. He makes me feel really good. I got a scholarship to play football and I just want to make him proud and carry on his name. People always ask me if I want to be like my dad, and truth is, yes—I want to be just like him. If I can be half the player he was, I'll be very successful. And I want to be just like him in every way, not just on the football field. Everybody loves him; he's such a caring person. Everyone in the city likes him; he's still talked about a lot. If I can be half the athlete and half the person he was and is, I'll be pretty good. I just love him and want to make him proud of me."

—Otis Taylor III, Otis's Son

•••

It was around my fifth year with the Chiefs, maybe later, when I tried illicit drugs for the first time. Somebody offered and, like most of the guys, I tried it. It was supposedly good and fun and all that other crap, but I found out that while it's good for a while, it gets worse. I was no different from anybody else, and the stuff was everywhere. Everywhere! I'd go into a restroom in a bar and, almost always, somebody would shout, "Big O!"

I'd look over and say, "What's up?"

"Do you want a toot of this? Do you want a toke of that?"

You know, very honestly, I'm a private person, and I wouldn't have taken it in a public place like that anyway. I usually said no, but I did indulge in it in situations like that during the course of my life. And, at one time, it got pretty bad. And then when I realized—learned, really—that if you smoke marijuana, if you mess with cocaine, it's going to get to you sooner or later. It's just a matter of time before it does. It's a very costly activity—and it got me.

I never gave anyone the line, "Well, I only did it twice." However many times you do it, the coke or pot or whatever, you've done it, and it's wrong. I knew it was wrong all along I suppose, but once I started doing the coke, smoking pot, and drinking more and more, I lost the handle I had on myself.

It's a wonder how and why certain things happen—one night I couldn't take it any more. I went outside, into my back yard. I was feeling sorry for myself, and I got down on my knees. I had never been a religious man, but I was drained of hope. I needed help. People have always told me, "Ask God to help. Ask God. He's the one who is able to make things happen." I was on my knees, and it was a nice night.

"God, please come into my life," I asked. "I need You. I'm not able to manage my life by myself. I can't do it, and I'm not ashamed that I can't do it.

"Come into my life and help me to do this, because I can't do it alone. I need your help." I asked God to give me the strength and right attitude to get rid of my problems.

I shed a couple of tears then, because my mama was still alive, and she used to tell me to pray all the time. I got up on my feet and looked around, and I was sweating—a clean sweat. I swear to God, I was sweating. Something had happened to me—I felt it, and I knew then I had the strength, at that moment in my backyard, to get my life right. It didn't happen right then, or even the next day. But I stopped soon after—the drugs, the drinking, even the cigarettes.

For more than 12 years I've been free from drugs and free from everything that I had ever tried, and that includes smoking. My son asked me to stop. He looked at me and said, "Dad, I don't want you to die from those cigarettes." I don't smoke or drink any more. People still offered me joints, lines and other stuff, and it was something that I had to work on. I'm no different from anybody else. It took control and willpower. I taste a little wine or something every now and then

My pride and joy, Otis III, as a basketball and football player at Raytown High School. (Photos courtesy of the Taylor Family Collection)

on a social basis. My drink used to be scotch—I probably should have bought stock in Chivas Regal because I know I spent enough money on it. But all that is gone, and I haven't had a desire for it.

I'm proud of myself—I was able to fight back and gain control of my life. My mother knew I had some problems when I called her and told her what happened to me in the back yard. She said, "I knew something was wrong. I just didn't know when I was going to ask you about the problems."

Everything high-powered in life that man has created, built or striven for, there's a woman somewhere behind him in his corner. I had to make a choice because I knew that after all those years my wife wasn't going to stand for me to keep doing the things that I was doing. I found the will and inner strength—or maybe it was given to me—to change. So, most of it is a mind trip, but that was a fight I needed to win—had to win.

14

WINNING

The only thing that I didn't do in the football world was to pull on a pair of khaki slacks and red shirt, stand on the sideline and coach. That was my dream, and it meant so much to me because I could still see myself involved, making things happen from the sideline. I get by myself sometimes and cry, wondering why it didn't happen, and that shows me I should forget. But it's not easy to forget something that you've held onto for years.

One day I was going to a Chiefs game and I needed to pick up my tickets. As I was going in the front door of the offices, a guy stopped me and said, "You can't go in there." Something hit me that day, and I turned to the guy, pointed to up to the stadium behind us, and snarled, "I built this goddamn thing. You see that brick up there? That's my brick. I helped build this goddamn place!" I waited for him to come back at me and say something else, because I was pissed. I stormed off. I shouldn't have done that. People don't know about the emotional pain I've had and the things that happened to me that I thought were wrong.

"Otis is well recognized. When people ask me when I played and I say back in the '60s, they ask, 'Is that when Lenny Dawson and Otis Taylor were playing?' I don't know why he isn't on those Hall of Fame ballots. He made some fabulous plays. Another thing is, for all these recent players, NFL Films did so much for them. If you played before NFL Films, you don't have that much of a chance to get anywhere because they kind of dictate that stuff. That's what the public sees and that's what everybody else sees. If you didn't play on Monday Night Football, people don't know who you are. That didn't come in until 1970. Anybody who played before then, you'll have to look in the history book to find them."

—Chris Burford

Here I am posing with Hank Stram, center, and Jan Stenerud, right, two Chiefs Hall of Famers. (Photo courtesy of the Taylor Family Collection)

The media in Kansas City and I always got along because I always tried to be as straightforward and truthful as I could. I understand that they don't sell papers by printing good things. And the people in Kansas City have always been true to me, and I think they deserve more than what they are getting as far as sports are concerned. The city is very high on its sports, especially football. Those people are crazy, and on game day they go berserk. They show a lot of love and care for the players, and they want to see a winner. They deserve to have a winner. I've always respected fans in KC, and I give them credit for being fair and honest. I've said it before: I love them. If I ever make it into the Hall of Fame, I hope every true fan in Kansas City can share it with me.

"It's amazing, he played so long ago, but people still want his autograph. That's the impression he left on the fans. It makes me feel good to hear and read all the nice and wonderful things that are said and written about him."

—Otis Taylor III

People can be overbearing when they ask for an autograph, but I know one day they'll stop asking. I sign every time I'm asked, and I've signed thousands. Black and white pictures, color prints, napkins, the shirt on their back—I've signed just about everything. People still want Otis Taylor's autograph, and the best part is that I get to hear their stories. A little old grandma—80 years old—asked for my autograph and then started crying, telling me that I was her first and only love. Perhaps a guy tells me how great it was to see us beat the Raiders in 1971, or maybe they were at the Christmas game against the Dolphins. If they saw me play, they tell me about their favorite catch. Sometimes people can be a little careless in the way they ask for an autograph. I have signed for some little kids who just walk off when I'm done.

"Come here," I'll say, and then, nodding, very politely tell them, "Thank you." The mom and dad are always standing there and they'll say, "Tell him, 'Thank you.'" I'm not trying to hurt the kids' feelings; I just want to make sure they learn their manners. They'll know the next time they ask for an autograph, and the next time might be an astronaut they meet at school. When he signs, the kid will thank him.

Learning the little things about life is important.

I feel I'm a blessed person. I haven't played football in a long time, but as long as you stay straight in Kansas City, you'll be thought of in a positive way. I've signed cards and memorabilia from people all over the country who say, "My mother told me about you," or "My grandpa loved to watch you play." And they always tell me I was one of the best players. One guy had a whole scrapbook of pictures of me.

I sign a lot of things for fans, something I'm always glad to do. (Photo courtesy of the Taylor Family Collection)

"I think Otis deserves to be in the Hall, but I don't know if people can look at his statistics and understand how good he was. Because when you look at receivers throughout the NFL history, I don't know a receiver who was better than Otis or more talented. But there were certainly guys with more statistics. I'd say there are two guys who should be in the Hall of Fame who'll maybe never get there—Curly Culp and Otis Taylor. If Otis can get there, I'll be very happy for him because he deserves it. He's that good."

—Mike Garrett

• • •

"There are so many people who know that Otis is my brother, even

though we are getting older. I say, 'That's Otis Taylor; he's my brother.' Everybody knows him and everybody respects him. If I need anything, all I have to do is call him or call his wife, and it's here. He's just the love of my life. He's all I've got now. My parents are gone, and it's just me and him."

—Florence Odell Taylor

About five years ago I found out I have Parkinson's disease. I didn't know anything about the disease at the time. I know almost everything about it now. It affects the nervous system, limiting a person's ability to control their muscles. This is caused by a slow, gradual loss of cells in the brain that produce a chemical called dopamine. For muscles to function normally, they must have dopamine. The disease causes a slight, involuntary shaking of the arms and legs—tremors. The muscles may feel stiff and rigid at times, making arm and leg movements difficult and slow. Eventually, a person's walking stride may become a slow process of taking small steps, which is called a shuffling gait.

My symptoms are up and down, and I usually take three pills a day, although I've had my medications changed a couple of times when things have gotten worse or better. This is a brain thing, and the pills slow it down and control the tremors. I'm never really in pain, but I do experience the stiffness a lot. I don't have any problem with my balance, and I can still get around okay. And of course, I'm hoping that in due time there will be enough progress made in the research field that something new will be available to help treat the disease. As it is now, everything else is all right. I mean, I can stand on one leg just as well as anybody else can and balance myself.

When I found out I had Parkinson's, I thought, "Damn, why did this happen to me?" I don't know if it's from the pounding I took on the football field or not. It doesn't matter. I don't have any shame

Here I am again with The Greatest, Muhammad Ali, this time in 1999. (Photo courtesy of the Taylor Family Collection)

about my condition, because one of the greatest men I have ever known—the greatest person I've ever touched and put my hand on—has Parkinson's, Muhammad Ali. And he's living life and making a contribution. So I'm not in it alone. I don't have problems speaking, but sometimes if I get excited when I'm talking, the tremors start. My wife works with me and she understands, and my son understands, too.

> "It is something to see. When we go out to a restaurant, someone always comes up to him and tells him how great they thought he was or that they loved to watch him play. And they always tell him that they think he should be in the Hall of Fame—we don't go anywhere without somebody saying that to him. I think it's a great honor that he receives the recognition and adulation of the Kansas City fans."

THE NEED TO WIN

—Regina Taylor

I hear it all the time: "Otis, why aren't you in the Hall of Fame?" And I don't know. I think I was a prototypical receiver during the time I played. I weighed 215-220 pounds, could run, catch, block, run over people when needed and make things happen after a run. I didn't run out of bounds. I think I should be in the group with Charlie Taylor or Fred Biletnikoff because I feel I did as much or more for my team as they did for theirs. I would rather be Otis Taylor with a championship under my belt and a Super Bowl ring with my great teammates than Lance Alworth—one of the best receivers ever—and in the Hall of Fame. I've heard the argument that I don't have the numbers. Well, football isn't all numbers, but I did catch 410 passes for 7,306 yards and I scored 60 touchdowns. And that was with a predominantly control-oriented, running-type team. When I played, most of the other teams in the league threw the ball about 100 times more per season than the Chiefs. Not that it's important, but if Lenny would have thrown the ball to me another 20 or 30 times a year, I'd have much larger numbers.

I need to put the Hall of Fame thing behind me now and stop thinking about it. It was getting to the point where I was worrying about it too much, and it had become too much a part of my life, and I have a whole lot of life to live. If I do get in one day, it will be one of the greatest moments and honors of my life to join people like Lenny Dawson, Willie Lanier, Bobby Bell, Hank Stram, Jan Stenerud, Buck Buchanan, Walter Payton and Lamar Hunt. It would be the ultimate honor. But what can I do about it? I did what I could do. I thought I performed at a high quality level during my playing days. I thought I did some special things on the football field. I was a big-time receiver and was considered the best at my position for four or five seasons. I made things happen, and I made a lot of people happy. If it happens, if the honor is extended to me, I hope it's before I leave this earth so I

John Madden selected me for his All-Time Super Bowl team in 1998. That's me hiding in the back row, third from the right behind Randy White and next to Mike Webster (No. 52). My teammate Willie Lanier is at the far left in the front row. (Photo courtesy of the Taylor Family Collection)

can enjoy the moment with my son, my wife, and my sister.

Not a day goes by without somebody in Kansas City asking me about the Hall of Fame, telling me their Super Bowl memories or just talking about football. This is every day of my life. It makes me feel good, because it feels like people really care about me. And how long has it been since I played? Almost 30 years and people are still talking about some of the things I did. Sometimes I can't believe it.

I've lived a good life, and maybe there are a few things that could have been different, but then I'm not going to bitch about that. I could have called this book *The Need to Fight,* because you have to fight, one way or another, to win. But really, I just hated to lose. It killed me to lose. I'm still trying to win and still need to win. Life is sweet today, and that's the important thing.

STATS

Otis Taylor, Jr.
Born: 8/11/42, Houston, TX
6'3" 215 lbs.
Prairie View A&M
Drafted: 1965, Round Four, Kansas City Chiefs

Year	TM	G	Att	Yards	Y/A	TD	Rec	Yards	Y/R	TD
			RUSHING				**RECEIVING**			
1965	KC	14	2	17	8.5	0	26	446	17.2	5
1966	KC	14	2	33	16.5	0	58	1297	22.4	8
1967	KC	14	5	29	5.8	1	59	958	16.2	11
1968	KC	11	5	41	8.2	1	20	420	21.0	4
1969	KC	11	2	-2	-1.0	0	41	696	17.0	7
1970	KC	13	3	13	4.3	0	34	618	18.2	3
1971	KC	14	1	25	25.0	1	57	1110	19.5	7
1972	KC	14	5	13	2.6	0	57	821	14.4	6
1973	KC	14	4	-14	-3.5	0	34	565	16.6	4
1974	KC	10	1	6	6.0	0	24	375	15.6	2
1975	KC	1	0	0	0.0	0	0	0	0.0	0
TOTAL		130	30	161	5.4	3	410	7306	17.8	57

SEASONS AMONG THE LEAGUE'S TOP 10

Receptions:	1966-3t*, 1967-4t*, 1971-3, 1972-3t
Receiving yards:	1966-2*, 1967-4*, 1971-1, 1972-5
Receiving TDs:	1965-10t*, 1966-4t*, 1967-1t*, 1969-6t*, 1971-5t
Yards from scrimmage:	1966-4*, 1967-9*, 1971-6
Rush/Receive TDs:	1966-10t*, 1967-2*, 1969-8t*

*AFL

Three-time Pro Bowler:	1966 (AFL), 1971, 1972
Postseason:	1966 and 1969 AFL Championship games Super Bowl I and Super Bowl IV